The Soul of Education

Helping Students Find Connection, Compassion, and Character at School

RACHAEL KESSLER

Association for Supervision and Curriculum Development
Alexandria, Virginia USA

Association for Supervision and Curriculum Development
1703 N. Beauregard St. • Alexandria, VA 22311-1714 USA
Telephone: 1-800-933-2723 or 703-578-9600 • Fax: 703-575-5400
Web site: http://www.ascd.org • E-mail: member@ascd.org

Gene R. Carter, *Executive Director*
Michelle Terry, *Associate Executive Director, Program Development*
Nancy Modrak, *Director, Publishing*
John O'Neil, *Director of Acquisitions*
Joan Halford, *Senior Associate Editor*
Julie Houtz, *Managing Editor of Books*
Carolyn Pool, *Associate Editor*
Laura Kelly, *Project Assistant*

Gary Bloom, *Director, Design and Production Services*
Karen Monaco, *Senior Designer*
Tracey A. Smith, *Production Manager*
Dina Murray, *Production Coordinator*
John Franklin, *Production Coordinator*
Valerie Sprague, *Desktop Publisher*
Winfield Swanson, *Indexer*

ASCD publications present a variety of viewpoints. The views expressed or implied in this book should not be interpreted as official positions of the Association.

Printed in the United States of America.

April 2000 member book (pcr). ASCD Premium, Comprehensive, and Regular members periodically receive ASCD books as part of their membership benefits. No. FY00-06.

ASCD Stock No. 100045
ASCD member price: $19.95   nonmember price: $23.95

Library of Congress Cataloging-in-Publication Data
Kessler, Rachael, 1946-
    The soul of education : helping students find connection, compassion, and character at school / Rachael Kessler.
        p. cm.
Includes bibliographical references and index.
"ASCD stock no. 100045"—T.p. verso.
    ISBN 0-87120-373-1 (pbk.)
   1. Affective education—United States. 2. Emotions—Study and teaching (Secondary)—United States. 3. Social skills—Study and teaching (Secondary)—United States. 4. Education Secondary—Activity
programs—United States. I. Title.
    LB1072+
    373.17'82—dc21   99-050911

05 04 03 02 01 00   10 9 8 7 6 5 4 3 2 1

The Soul of Education

Helping Students Find Connection, Compassion, and Character at School

*In memory of those brilliant young souls for whom
it might have been different, and on behalf
of so many today for whom it still can be.*

Foreword

By Parker J. Palmer

During the Great Depression of the 1930s, folk singer Woody Guthrie wrote and recorded an instant classic called "The Talkin' Dust Bowl Blues." Among its many bittersweet lines is this one: "That soup was so thin you could read a magazine through it."

The 20th century, for all its scientific and technological amazements, might be described as a century of thin soup, and not only because too many people went hungry. It was a century in which we watered down our own humanity—turning wisdom into information, community into consumerism, politics into manipulation, destiny into DNA—making it increasingly difficult to find nourishment for the hungers of the heart.

Education has not been exempt from this process. Early in the century, eager to create factory workers who could produce material prosperity, we took teaching and learning—that ancient exchange between student and teacher and world in which human beings have always explored the depths of the soul—and started thinning it down into little more than the amassing of data and the mastering of technique.

That's the bad news. The good news is that the educational soup became so thin—and our hunger for real life so deep—that in the last decades of the 20th century people started seeing right through it. Teachers, administrators, parents, and citizens who care about education have been working hard to reclaim the integrity of teaching and learning so that it can once again become a process in which the whole person is nourished.

Parker J. Palmer is a writer, teacher, and activist who lives in Madison, Wisconsin. His most recent books are *The Courage to Teach: Exploring the Inner Landscape of a Teacher's Life* and *Let Your Life Speak: Listening for the Voice of Vocation.*

If you are, or want to become, part of this ongoing effort, you will find no better resource than the volume you hold in your hands. *The Soul of Education* is a remarkable book. It offers a compelling vision of depth in education. It is grounded in encouraging stories of practice from the real world of teaching and learning. And it was written by a teacher's teacher. Rachael Kessler understands the dynamics of teaching and learning, the deepest needs of our children, the longings of our own adult hearts, and what will be required of us if we are to reclaim our humanity in 21st century life.

This book calls not only for changes in classroom practice but for a new direction in our national conversation about educational reform. Many of us who care about public education are disheartened by the "fixes" put forward by our political leaders. They too often promote simplistic answers that attempt to change education from the outside in—such as establishing one-size-fits-all "standards" to which students and teachers must measure up or be judged as failures.

Standards are important in education, of course, but the standards soup is now so thin that we can see some of its sad consequences: teachers preparing students for the test rather than for their lives; teachers helping their students cheat on the test, knowing that the standards can never be achieved honestly with the resources at hand; states whose scores are a public embarrassment surreptitiously lowering the standards or abandoning them altogether.

Kessler's book does not ignore the standards movement, but responds creatively to the deeper yearning behind it: the desire to truly engage and equip today's young people for effective learning. We must address what has heart and meaning for them if we want them to learn. *The Soul of Education* is replete with concrete examples of how to do so.

In "The Talkin' Dust Bowl Blues," the line, "That soup was so thin you could read a magazine through it," ends with these words: "If it had been any thinner, some of them politicians could' a seen right through it." If all of us, leaders and followers alike, would embrace the principles of soulful teaching and learning that Rachael Kessler advocates so convincingly in this book, we would neither tolerate nor promote an education that ignores the inner life. This book will give us eyes to see through the fictions that diminish our public schools today. It will give us the courage to create new forms of authentic education that can contribute to the healing of souls—our children's, our own, and the world's.

Acknowledgments

A wide circle of educators, students, and friends has made this book possible. First, I want to thank the thousands of students and teachers with whom I have worked these past 20 years who have shared their stories, their questions, and their creative ideas about how to nurture the soul of students. I am particularly grateful to those who took an interest in this book and came by to share their thoughts.

Many educators and scholars were generous with their time and ideas through interviews and correspondence. Colleen Conrad, Doug Eaton, and Chip Wood allowed me to return to the well many times. Others shared their unpublished writing, their thoughts, and their contacts: Howard Gardner, Parker Palmer, Douglas Sloan, Linda Lantieri, Jack Miller, Laura Simms, Chris Gerzon, Mary Lou Faddick, Jeffrey Duvall, Karen Halverson, Joy Guarino, Mark Hartwig, Heather Koerner, Gary Comstock, Jackie Adolph, Elissa Weindling, Jacqueline Norris, Phil Morse, Susan Heinbauch, Risa Marlin, Sandy Parker, Kathy Leo, Jill Miller, Nancy Jane, and Linda Bruehne. My colleagues at the Collaborative for the Advancement of Social and Emotional Learning (CASEL), especially Maurice Elias, Mark Greenberg, Norris Haynes, Tim Shriver, and Roger Weissberg, offered support in the early stages of the book. And I will always be grateful to Paul Cummins, founder of the Crossroads School, and to Jack Zimmerman of the Ojai Foundation for their courage in initiating a curriculum that incubated so many of the practices and principles offered in this book.

Critical readers from across the political spectrum enriched this book and supported my efforts to create a bridge of understanding and respect between constituencies in education who have long suffered estrangement and polarization. I feel immensely blessed by Perry Glanzer, former education and religious liberty analyst for Focus on the Family, who read and responded to each chapter in the early stages to help me understand and respect the point of view of traditionalist Christian educators. Chip Wood, cofounder of the Northeast Foundation for Children, was also a careful reader of early drafts, offering support and insights that strengthened the book.

The financial and moral support of the Fetzer Institute, the Compton Foundation, and Richard Chasin made it possible for me to devote the time and peace of mind essential to researching and writing this book. Ron and Susan Kertzner opened their hearts and home to provide a sanctuary in which to write. My dear friends Claudia Gvirtzman, Jude Blitz and Tom Daly, and Bill and Lizanne Ury gave me courage during the hard times. I am also grateful to John Steiner, who has provided careful guidance, and to Michael Lerner, who offered bridges to so many worlds that ultimately made this book possible.

I also wish to thank those who have nurtured me as a writer. My mother, Pauline Kessler, inspired in me a devotion to writing by her example and her dreams. For close to a decade, my agent and friend, Jill Kneerim, has guided me to stay true to my vision and voice for this book. Ron Miller, my first editor, has helped me grow immensely in both skill and confidence as a writer. I deeply appreciate the generosity of my colleague, Katia Borg, who created the logo for each of the seven gateways. And the team at ASCD has called forth my best with their respect, encouragement, and toughness. I could not have imagined in a publishing house the personal care and support I have received.

Finally, I would like to thank my family. Each of my sons—Shane, Ari, and Mikael Gerzon-Kessler—contributed their wisdom and stories to this book and a deep well of love and encouragement to its author. And my husband, partner, and fellow author, Mark Gerzon, has challenged and supported me in many ways to hone my skills as a writer and to follow my vision and mission as an educator who was determined to discover what it meant to nurture soul in education.

RACHAEL KESSLER
Boulder, Colorado
March 2000

Introduction

A book entitled *The Soul of Education* inevitably raises the question "Should modern public school education even *have* a soul?"

Geometry and history, English and science—places and times for these subjects in the contemporary classroom are secure. But the *soul*? Doesn't that belong in church? Aren't questions of the soul private, spiritual matters that are best left at home?

If so, someone had better tell the children. While we adults continue to debate these questions, most students continue to bring their souls to school. Except for the very few who are so deadened by drugs, abuse, or neglect that their inner lives are numb, students of all ages come to school with their souls alive and seeking connection.

The question *"Does a child's soul have a place in the classroom?"* leads beyond yes or no. If we say "no," it leads to the untenable conclusion that modern schooling is soulless. But if we say "yes," it immediately ignites a firestorm of further questions—four of which we must explore now:

- What *is* soul, anyway? Whose definition are we using?
- However we define it, can educators and parents come together to find ways to invite soul into education?
- Doesn't the U.S. constitutional requirement of "separation of church and state" mean leaving all this alone?
- How do we as teachers nourish spiritual development in school?

The power of these questions to trigger strong, polarized reactions shows that, even in our secular, high-tech world, our spirits hunger for answers. To me, the most important challenge has always been not *whether* we can address spiritual development in secular schools but *how*.

What Does "Soul of Education" Mean?

When soul is present in education, attention shifts. As the quality of attention shifts, we listen with great care not only to what people say but to the messages between the words—tones, gestures, the flicker of feeling across the face. And then we concentrate on what has heart and meaning. The yearning, wonder, wisdom, fear, and confusion of students become central to the curriculum. Questions become as important as answers.

When soul enters the classroom, masks drop away. Students dare to share the joy and talents they have feared would provoke jealousy in even their best friends. They risk exposing the pain or shame that peers might judge as weakness. Seeing deeply into the perspective of others, accepting what has felt unworthy in themselves, students discover compassion and begin to learn about forgiveness.

The body of the child will not grow if it is not fed; the mind will not flourish unless it is stimulated and guided. And the spirit will suffer if it is not nurtured. A soulful education embraces diverse ways to satisfy the spiritual hunger of today's youth. When guided to find constructive ways to express their spiritual longings, young people can find purpose in life, do better in school, strengthen ties to family and friends, and approach adult life with vitality and vision.

Clearly, this is not a metaphysical definition of soul or spirit. To engage those questions would take us into the realm of belief and dogma. While entirely appropriate for philosophy or religious education, basing curriculum on any particular definition of soul would inevitably divide us and violate the worldview of one group or another. For this reason, I use the word *soul* in this book to call for attention in schools to the inner life; to the depth dimension of human experience; to students' longings for something more than an ordinary, material, and fragmented existence.

Can We Come Together to Address Soul in Schools?

Educators are beginning to refer to a "spiritual problem" in our culture, scholars analyzing school violence speak of "spiritual emptiness," and members of Congress struggling for solutions lament the "spiritual darkness" that afflicts the young. A consensus is emerging that some kind of spiritual void exists for youth—and we must address it. As Warren Nord (1995) writes:

> We modern day Americans have a spiritual problem. There is something fundamentally wrong with our culture. We who have succeeded so brilliantly in matters of economics, science, and technology have been less successful in matters of the heart and soul. This is evident in our manners and our morale; in our entertainment and our politics; in our preoccupation with sex and violence; in the ways we do our jobs and in the failure of our relationships; in our boredom and unhappiness in this, the richest of all societies (p. 380).

Naturally, our schools reflect this problem. But can we face together the question of nourishing soul in the classroom, or is it too tendentious to allow us to move forward?

I believe that we are better able to meet this challenge now than at any time in our history. On the one hand, the diversity of faiths and nonfaiths today in most school communities is so overwhelming that no single denomination could possibly be appropriate as an official, or even unofficial, school religion. On the other hand, with even physicists and astronomers joining in the quest for answers to the age-old questions about the meaning of life, educators can no longer pretend that banning spiritual questions from school property is feasible. And there is a growing awareness among parents and educators that a spiritual void is endangering our youth and our communities.

In the United States, we have had a series of "prevention wars" on drugs, teen pregnancy, youth suicide, and violence (Shriver & Weissberg, 1996). But the spiritual void—the emptiness, meaningless, and disconnection many students feel—is a root cause long left out of the analysis and the cure. Only recently, and particularly after the tragic epidemic of schoolyard massacres of the late 1990s, are policymakers and social scientists beginning to recognize our neglect of the souls of young people in schools and in our national life (Benson, 1997; "Kids Who Kill," 1999). "I think that's a very important part of all of this, the spiritual emptiness that so many kids feel," said Cornell professor James Garbarino when a panel of experts sought understanding on the day following the Columbine massacre in Littleton, Colorado. "And when they feel it, when things go bad in their lives, there's nothing to fall back on and also there's no limits to their behavior" ("Kids Who Kill," 1999).

Similarly, as a House subcommittee responded to the eruption of violence plaguing our youth, Congressman Tom Tancredo (R, 6th, CO) spoke of "a spiritual darkness that permeates the moral landscape of the nation." A member of the House Education Committee, Tancredo

xii   *The Soul of Education*

continued: "Our task is to now forgo cursing its existence and begin to light the candles that will pierce it" (cited in Romano, 1999, pp. 4, 11).

Although we must address the socioeconomic sources of the persistent violent and self-destructive behavior of our teenagers, we cannot really understand or heal from these plagues if we do not begin to recognize and meet the spiritual needs of our children. Do we need periodic reminders from sawed-off shotguns to show us that these young people *feel*? Is it possible that these senseless acts of violence are guiding us back to what, in our hearts, we know is a core mission of education in the first place?

Perhaps we do need these reminders. Many communities decided years ago that the inner life of our children was simply not the business of public schools. Many classrooms are "spiritually empty," not by accident, *but by design.*

We decided to exclude the spiritual dimension from education because we adults couldn't agree on what "it" was or how to teach "it." Liberals fear that "fundamentalists" will sue them as "New Agers" if they introduce a spiritual dimension into the classroom. Christians fear that secularists will paralyze their efforts to provide spiritual guidance to children in schools. Other religious groups are often not even included in the conversation. Collectively, we reached a standoff, and our children have been the losers.

Many communities have decided that the inner lives of our young people in the public schools wouldn't be *anybody's* business. Seeking a respectful way to deal with our differences, we educators turned away from matters of religion and spirituality. Of course, many teachers, schools, and communities are devoted to serving the social, emotional, moral, and even spiritual needs of students (Elias et al., 1997). But when schools systematically exclude heart and soul, students in growing numbers become depressed, attempt suicide, or succumb to eating disorders and substance abuse. Students struggle to find their motivation to learn, to stay in school, or to keep their attention on what is before them. And straight-*A* students drive BMWs on their way to shooting fellow students and attempting to incinerate their school with explosives. Welcoming soul into the classroom is not a panacea for all these ills; but it is crucial for addressing the suffering of our youth.

Until recently, educators would have met the subject of this book primarily with fear. Exploring spiritual development in schools, educators have feared, will bring down the wrath of people who will vilify them, sue them, and take away their jobs. But something is changing.

Educators and social scientists are asking, "How can we fill the spiritual void?" because they see students destroying themselves and each other. Others have personally glimpsed the riches of the inner life in the wave of spiritual search and renewal among adults in the 1990s. Both groups are asking, "How can we appropriately address our students' spiritual growth in ways that do not violate the beliefs of families or the separation of church and state?"

My own work has been informed by two impulses: a desire to prevent violence and a desire to honor the spiritual yearnings in young people. I began my work with adolescents in the field of prevention—seeking to create curriculums and methods that would address the root causes of suffering in a "generation at risk." Working with teenagers, I also discovered an exquisite opening to spirit at the heart of the adolescent experience. Adolescence is a time when longings awaken with an intensity that many have misunderstood and dismissed as "hormones." The larger questions about meaning, identity, responsibility, and purpose begin to press with an urgency and loneliness we can all remember. Ignored or suppressed, the spiritual forces inside our young turn toxic and explosive. Providing students with opportunities to channel their energy constructively and to explore their mysteries with peers and supportive elders, I saw young people find balance, integrity, meaning, and connection.

The fears of integrating a spiritual dimension into the classroom have not gone away. But a broad cross-section of U.S. citizens now urgently wants to tend to the souls of our young people. Nowhere is this need stronger than among educators. When ASCD devoted an entire issue of *Educational Leadership* to "The Spirit of Education" (1998/1999), the editors received a windfall of unsolicited manuscripts of outstanding quality and won a Bronze Excel Award from the Society for National Association Publications for the issue. This journal has begun a long-overdue conversation that we can no longer postpone—a rare open moment in our field and in our culture to speak what has been unspeakable for decades.

The quest for soul in education can move forward only in communities where educators, parents, and civic leaders are willing to air their deepest differences in a spirit of dialogue and collaboration. This book provides dozens of practical examples of how educators actually welcome soul into the classroom.

Doesn't the "Separation of Church and State" Mean Leaving All This Alone?

One reason we have excluded any spiritual dimension from public education is a mistaken belief that this is required by the "separation of church and state." The First Amendment to the Constitution of the United States protects public school children from the imposition of any particular worldview or religious practices. Any teacher who espouses spiritual beliefs or who conducts devotional practices in the classroom is indeed violating the "non-establishment" clause. At the same time, the First Amendment protects the rights of our children to *freely express their own beliefs*. Many teachers have tried to be so vigilant about keeping religion out of the classroom that they have unknowingly violated the rights of their students. It has become common practice for teachers to suppress student expression or exploration of their own beliefs, longings, or search for a spiritually meaningful experience.

We do need to be careful. If we define spirituality in terms of beliefs that one group holds and others do not, we violate the First Amendment by imposing such beliefs through curriculums in public schools. It is true that for many adults, spirituality is inextricably linked with their particular faith and doctrines. Listening to students for many years, however, has shown me that young people have experiences that nourish their spiritual development and *yet are not directly related to worldview or religious dogma*. We *can* honor the First Amendment without abandoning our children's spiritual development.

How Do We Nourish Spiritual Development Appropriately in Public Schools?

As we approached the millennium, the field of education began to discover the vital relationships among teaching, learning, and the education of the heart. Building on the earlier concepts of "intrapersonal" and "interpersonal intelligence" framed by Howard Gardner (1993), Daniel Goleman (1994) documented that "emotional intelligence" is a greater predictor of academic and life success than is IQ. Goleman introduced the concept of "emotional literacy"—a "shorthand term for the idea that children's emotional and social skills can be cultivated, and that doing so gives them decided advantages in their cognitive abilities, in their personal adjustment, and in their resiliency through life" (p. 33). This definition, and the solid research in his groundbreaking book, *Emotional Intelligence* (1995), gave educators a language and legitimacy for an aspect of education that has often been little understood or respected. In the same year, Robert Sylwester's work, *A Celebration of Neurons,* introduced the larger educational community to the implications of recent brain theory and research for schooling. "Emotion is very important to the educative process," wrote Sylwester (1995, p. 72), "because it drives attention, which drives learning and memory."

It is a small, but crucial step from the education of the heart to *The Soul of Education.* Nothing could be more "emotion laden" in a positive sense than the experiences that students recount as nourishing to their souls. As we face this question—"How can we nourish spiritual development in school?"—the fields of social and emotional learning, brain-based learning, and intelligence theory have been extremely useful. But they do not answer the question. The answer to this question comes from no textbook, existing research, or metaphysical treatise. Rather it begins in the hearts of the boys and girls, the young women and young men, who sit in classrooms in every community. For more than two decades, my colleagues and I have been listening to what young people wonder about themselves, about each other, and about the universe itself. I believe that, if we start with them, the answer to the question of "how" may emerge more clearly.

Over many years, my passion has been to understand what feeds the spirit of young people and to create curriculum, methodology, and teacher development that would serve this need. After working for several years in social policy on children's issues and then developing programs for teenage mothers in Massachusetts, I was hired in 1985 to chair a Department of Human Development at an innovative private school in Santa Monica, California. I led a team in creating the first curriculum for adolescents that integrated heart, spirit, and community with a strong academic curriculum at this highly successful college preparatory school. We designed a curriculum called the "Mysteries Program,"[1] in response to the "mysteries" of teenagers: their usually unspoken questions and concerns.

In the 1990s I expanded this approach, including what I had learned from many colleagues in the field of social and emotional learning. Renaming this curriculum the "Passages Program," I have brought this perspective into public and private schools. Whereas my own experience comes through courses for adolescents designated for social and emotional learning, the principles and methods that

---

[1]The Mysteries Program was initiated by Jack Zimmerman under the leadership of headmaster Paul Cummins at the Crossroads School in Santa Monica, California.

emerged have since been integrated by teachers into all grade levels and subject areas.

After listening to thousands of students, both my own and those of my colleagues from around the country, I began to hear a pattern. In their stories and questions, young people celebrate the dimensions of life that satisfied their souls:

> The beauty, the majesty—it's indescribable, the power I feel inside when I'm deep in the forest or walking along a rushing river.

> I was the geek, the dork you all made fun of. I'm still not cool. I know it. But you guys have really taken me in; you've accepted me, you've respected me. I know how far you've come.

> There is something that happens to me in pottery class—I lose myself in the feeling of wet clay rolling smoothly under my hands as the wheel spins. I have it last period, so no matter how difficult the day was, pottery makes every day a good day. It's almost magical—to feel so good, so serene.

Over and over, students identified certain experiences as precious and meaningful to them. In my mind, a map of seven gateways to the soul of students began to emerge (see Chapter 1). Each subsequent chapter is devoted to one of these gateways. Through the stories of students and educators, these chapters explore the risks and opportunities of creating ways to invite these experiences into the classroom.

From the outset, however, I want to distinguish between two kinds of experiences: (1) "religious education" and "devotional practices" and (2) ordinary experiences that can nourish spiritual development. Here, I focus on the latter. I provide both a theoretical framework and a wide range of concrete activities for students, teachers, and parents that respect the diverse belief systems and cultures present in our classrooms.

I could never have developed this framework or these methods alone. Like any educator, I have my own biography and biases. To create this approach to spiritual development while respecting diverse points of view, I have been blessed with the guidance and support of a diverse group of colleagues—secular, holistic, and Christian educators and theorists. All have sensitized me to the different, often seemingly polarized, convictions that must be respected by educators who seek a place for soul in the classroom. Along with the stories of students and teachers, the insights and warnings of these varying perspectives appear throughout the book.

The teachers who provided many of the book's stories and examples have found ways to cultivate soul in their classes while respecting the content of their particular curriculum. Teachers of math, science, English, foreign languages, and social studies have all used the methods described here. Once teachers have a framework for supporting the spiritual dimension of their students' growth, they are remarkably inventive in developing new ways for doing so. When I use stories from these teachers, I use full names for those who chose to share their stories and insights with me specifically for this book. When I use first names only, I am protecting anonymity for teachers who spoke with no knowledge of my writing.

In addition to the counsel of fellow educators, this framework has profoundly benefitted from the thousands of students with whom I have worked. The map of the seven gateways described in this work grows directly out of their statements and stories, their questions and yearnings. Although I have changed the names of all students to protect their privacy, the hundreds of student voices in these pages represent actual students, taught by me or by my colleagues. I have not created composites or fictional characters. Within the limits of memory, the student voices come from specific young people.

Meet now a few of the scores of students who speak out in this book:

• A high school senior, dying of cancer, gives her classmates an opportunity to face the reality of suffering and celebrate life;
• A high school girl immersed in hatred for herself and others discovers her capacity for love amidst the acceptance she feels in a classroom community;
• A boy whose critique of a class is taken seriously and respected by his teacher discovers his own capacities for leadership and then runs successfully for school president;
• A boy who has been slighted by his father as a loser, in comparison to his successful older brother, is embraced by his dad in a ceremony that allows the barriers between them to finally come down.

The inner life of these and other young people is intimately bound up with matters of meaning, purpose, and connection, with creative expression and moments of joy and transcendence. All these qualities are central to both emotional intelligence and to constructively filling the spiritual void. Classroom environments that acknowledge and invite such experiences help students break down stereotypes, improve discipline, increase academic motivation, foster creativity, and keep more kids in school. Let us dare to consider together the possibilities and pitfalls of consciously honoring in school the inner lives of our students.

1
Honoring Young Voices

I am teaching a class for seniors that is designed to be a rite of passage from adolescence to adulthood. Two-thirds of the way through the semester, we travel from our school to a retreat center in the mountains of Ojai, several hours away. We camp in an oak grove, creating opportunities for private reflection, for play, and for facing common challenges.

Now it's the last day of the retreat, and we are preparing for our closing ceremony. Suddenly I realize that Felicia, a beautiful but brittle 17-year-old student who is struggling with the final stages of bone cancer, will never make it down the hill on her crutches. She staunchly refuses our help. Except for hourly injections of painkillers that my colleague is giving her, she acts as if she wants to face death alone.

As her teacher, I want to respect Felicia's strength and not injure her pride. At the same time, I feel that she has reached that stage in her illness and her life where she needs to accept help. Because everyone wants to include Felicia at this ceremony, leaving her behind isn't an option.

Bewildered, I sit down on a rock and take a moment to reflect. What are we going to do? How can I help this dying young woman inspire her peers with her indomitable strength, while also learning—for the first and last time in her life—to accept support from others?

❧ ❧ ❧

Felicia joined our class in the spring despite her frail condition. She had been diagnosed with cancer in the 10th grade, and she spent much of her junior year away from school seeking cures anywhere her devoted parents could find hope. She was so weak this year, she could

1

hardly attend classes. By spring, she was on painkillers around the clock, she could walk only with the support of crutches, and her energy was almost gone. But she was determined about one thing: She would participate in this senior rite of passage.

"She wants so much to be normal," her mother confided in me. "She is so independent—she always has been. And she wants to participate just like the others. She knows that this is her chance to separate from us as well—to become a grown-up. She needs so much to do this, I can't tell you how much it means to her."

Working closely with Felicia's parents was essential because the advanced state of her cancer involved problematic issues of medication, transportation, and potential emergency care.

When we left on the school bus for the mountain retreat center, I told my students that Felicia's parents would do their best to bring her. The exuberance of the students as they settled into the retreat was tempered by fear and grief. Felicia was a crucial part of this group that had worked toward the retreat with great anticipation after the wildly enthusiastic stories of previous seniors. Would she have to miss this experience? And if she did come, how would they deal with it?

❧ ❧ ❧

In our opening "council" meeting on the first afternoon of the retreat, we passed a round loaf of bread, with each of the 22 students in turn tearing off a piece and stating what nourishment they hoped to receive during the next five days and the nourishment they hoped to give. But then one of the students broke down. "I want so much to give my love to Felicia—I know we don't have much time left, and there's so much I want to tell her. But I feel like I shouldn't talk about it—like she'll know if I get emotional that I know she's dying and we're not supposed to ever think that. I'm supposed to pretend everything's okay. But it's not okay. Sure, I keep praying that she'll make it somehow. But I have eyes. Don't you?" she looked around the room at the faces filled with tears.

Her outburst then triggered another student: "This is my senior retreat," he said. "My special time. I've been thinking about this for four years now. I've got so much going on—so many decisions to make, so many goodbyes. How am I going to take care of all this if I'm worrying about Felicia? I feel selfish saying this, even thinking this. But I know we're supposed to be honest here. If I can't be honest here, where can I be?"

"How do we treat her now?" wondered a third student. "She wants us to act like everything's cool, but it's not. What do we do with *our* sadness and our fear when we're with her?

"And she won't let us help her in any way. It seems so dishonest. I mean, she needs us. And we need her—she knows things about life we need to learn from her. But can we really talk straight with her about all this? It seems so impossible."

As her best friend May sobbed with grief during this council, I felt grateful that Felicia was not here. It was an opportunity to speak with the students about life and death on a deeper level than any of us had expected.

"We are all so busy trying to take care of Felicia that we have not really tended to our own pain," I began. "This pain of watching your friend dying is yours—and it comes when you already have so much to deal with—making huge decisions, preparing to leave all that's been secure and familiar for you. And in the midst, you are carrying this enormous pain."

I felt the room relax as I named and honored their suffering.

"We have to really take care of each other these next few days," I continued, my own voice shaken by tears. "If Felicia comes, we need to remember to take care of each person here, even as we do our best to care for her."

"Felicia's here," one of my students shouted, as we sat around the campfire before the evening council. I jumped up.

When I arrived at the kitchen, Felicia was waiting impatiently to join the group. Her father and mother had driven her up the dirt road usually closed to cars in this beautiful mountain retreat center.

"How wonderful that you're here!" I said, embracing her awkwardly, around her crutches. "Thank you so much, Mr. Sanchez, for bringing her. We have all been eager to share this time with Felicia."

"Don't thank me," he replied humbly. "We are most grateful to you all for making it possible for our girl to be here." Then I embraced her mother, Ruth, who had become a friend from our many dialogues about her daughter.

"Let's go join the others," I said, beckoning to Felicia. "And you're welcome to join us, too," I encouraged her parents. Felicia glared at them to let them know she was determined to do this alone.

"You'll have to be careful with those crutches, Felicia—it's a bumpy, rocky path," I warned. Her father rushed to assist her, and she pushed him away, angrily.

The other students were ecstatic when Felicia arrived at the fire. Swept up in a wave of whoops and hugs, she melted into the group.

For the next four days, we explored the challenges of navigating the critical passage from childhood to adulthood. In council meetings, students shared their hopes, their fears, their gratitude, and their regrets; gradually, these students found their way to confronting honestly and tenderly some of their most difficult feelings with Felicia. Their reflections about death were perhaps the most courageous and thoughtful I have ever seen expressed by people of any age.

During free time, they explored the land and organized major campaigns of "Capture the Flag" and "Ultimate Frisbee." We challenged them to spend hours alone—listening to the wind in the trees and to their own hearts. We created enactments of the journey of letting go and embracing their strengths and their futures. Felicia participated as much as possible—resting when exhaustion overtook her, but maintaining a strong presence in our group.

We planned our closing ceremony quite spontaneously. During their free time the students had found a beautiful spot down the hill from our meeting rooms, far past the sleeping grounds. In the exuberance of the moment, we teachers agreed, not thinking of how difficult it would be for Felicia to get there. Now we have to confront this problem.

Suddenly I have an idea. I approach a group of boys hanging out together and lower my voice. "Would one of you guys be willing to carry Felicia down the hill if we need you?" Two young men volunteer immediately. One—Jimmy—is probably our tallest, strongest student. He also has a reputation outside this class for being a good-for-nothing cut-up. He has been a disappointment to his father, who had raised him and an older brother, who was a star athlete and academic success. But in our work in this class, Jimmy has proved himself trustworthy, even of this delicate task. Since the first day of the semester, Jimmy has seen this class as a place that was safe enough to expose his pain, his longing, his wisdom. Our group has loved and acknowledged the beauty of this struggling young man.

I ask Jimmy and Will, the other volunteer, to go inside. Then I ask Felicia and her best friend, May, to join me for a moment in our meeting room.

"Felicia, you have a choice to make. The walk we're about to take is too far for you to do on crutches. Would you be comfortable letting either Jimmy or Will carry you on his shoulders? It would mean a lot to these guys and to all of us if you would accept our help." Our days together have made it easier for her to face the truth, to let go, and to let us in. But still she hesitates. She cannot decide.

"Do it, Licia!" May says, gleefully. "You can ride on Jimmy, and I'll ride on Will. We'll be side by side, riding in style. It will feel like a parade!"

Felicia's eyes light up with a girlish joy I had seen only in photos from before the cancer. "Yes!" she shouts, high-fiving May, and then Will and Jimmy. "Let's do it—it will be a blast!"

The rest of us tromp behind them down the hill as Felicia and May ride like prom queens on the shoulders of these proud young boys-becoming-men. They are carrying her for all of us—allowing her to surrender to our love and care.

In our hearts we all know that this is truly a moment of "passage" for Felicia—and for all of us. Despite our continuing hopes and prayers that this young senior will make it to graduation, we sense that a much more challenging graduation awaits her.

A month later, on her 18th birthday, Felicia died.

⚘ ⚘ ⚘

Fortunately, most high school classes do not wrestle so immediately with death. Nor do they have the privilege of five days in the magic of mountains. But in most secondary classrooms, adolescents everywhere are carrying the profound questions that challenged Felicia's group. *What gives meaning to life? Why am I here? Can I ask for help? Does anyone really love me?* The teenage years are a time when the most important questions can fester in loneliness—or with support, inspire a journey toward wisdom and connection.

When a group of students can acknowledge the truth, whether it is malevolent or benign, when they can meet where their personal stories strike universal chords, they become a community that can respond constructively to any challenge—even death. This is the soul of education.

But *how* do educators begin to make a place for soul in the classroom? What does it mean to nourish the spiritual development of adolescents in school?

There is little in the educational literature to answer these questions. For me, both the questions and the answers have emerged from my day-to-day work with students.

As I developed this work in the 1980s, I sensed that it was meeting student needs at a very deep level; but I didn't know then what to call it. For several years, I thought it was best not to try. Like most educators, I thought it would be too dangerous to acknowledge that we were doing something in school that involved the spiritual dimension. In the mid-'80s, educators did not dare to consider or discuss the possibility that soul might have a place in schools. If we had used the words "spiritual" or "soul," some students would have thought it was "hokey" or "flaky." Others would have felt we were intruding. Parents and colleagues might have heard the word "spirit" and assumed we were proselytizing or practicing devotional exercises that violated their personal beliefs and the First Amendment as well.

I could not explain what it was about the Mysteries classes that invited soul into the room. We were not practicing religion or even talking about religion. Though I was eager to understand, I did not seek answers from books or spiritual teachers. I was determined to learn *from my students*. Because I wanted to find a pure, fresh, direct connection to what nourished the human spirit, I decided to listen to the voices of the young people themselves.

Teenagers, however, do not readily share what is deeply important with anyone, certainly not with most adults called "teachers." To earn their trust, I had to learn ways to work together to create an environment that was safe and full of respect and compassion so that they would speak with authenticity. The more they felt their voices honored by their peers and teacher, the more they were willing to speak.

I discovered four practices that proved crucial to inviting soul into the classroom:

• *A ground rules process* that empowers students to define and take ownership of the conditions for safety in their group.

• *Games and symbolic expressions* that offer teenagers an indirect way to express themselves and meet each other gradually in deeper, more personal ways.

• *The "mysteries questions" process*, underscoring that we will be talking about what is in the hearts of these particular students, not someone else's "curriculum."

• *The council process*, which enables students to listen and speak from the heart, telling stories about what matters most to them.

These practices were the steppingstones on my path to discovering a safe, responsible, and effective way to make a place for soul in the classroom. Each was based on the principle of honoring young voices.

Ground Rules

I could never have begun my journey without giving students a way to define the conditions they most needed to speak about their longings and concerns.

"Together, we can make this class a place where it's possible to talk about what is really important to *you*," I say to my students once they have begun to feel comfortable with our class. (I usually wait until the second or third class, using the first classes to establish comfort and connection with activities that require little risk or self-revelation.) "Our curriculum comes from your issues, your questions, and your challenges as you go through this time of your lives. But if you're going to risk speaking about what really matters personally, what do you need—from yourself and from others—to make it safe to do that?"

"Trust." Invariably, this word comes out first.

"Yes, trust is essential. But what is it that would allow you to trust others, and to trust yourself? Most of us are pretty cautious when we begin to reveal what really matters to us. I think that's healthy, don't you? I don't want to encourage you to trust for the sake of trust. Blind trust can be naive and dangerous. We always have to be discerning. What actions, what behaviors tell us we can begin to trust?"

They begin to call out words, and I stand at the board listening and writing.

"Respect."

"Honesty."

"No put-downs."

"Listening as if you really want to know."

"No laughing at people."

"No interruptions."

"Don't make judgments."

"An open mind."

"Trust."

"Respect for my privacy."[1]

"The right to stay quiet and speak only when I'm ready."

Thousands of students across the United States create this same list again and again—from 7th grade through high school.[2] The language may vary, but the sentiments are the same. Differences may deeply divide this nation, but I find widespread agreement among teenagers

---

[1]Confidentiality is a thorny and complex issue for teachers, students, and parents. I have explored the limits to confidentiality in depth in "The Dilemma of Confidentiality," available on the Web site of the Institute for Social and Emotional Learning (http://www.mediatorsfoundation.org/soulofed). See also the discussion of "Pandora's Box" in Chapter 6, which addresses reporting suspected abuse.

[2]Some form of collaborative agreement process is fundamental to most programs in social and emotional learning. See Elias et al. (1997), *Promoting Social and Emotional Learning: Guidelines for Educators*.

(and among adults) when it comes to defining what makes it possible to speak authentically.

Once the students and teacher have collaboratively established ground rules, they can begin to move toward genuine communication.

Games and Symbolic Expression

Trust builds slowly. After all, I am asking students to begin to dissolve some of the boundaries between their private feelings and the public life of school. Unlike participants in a weekly youth group outside of school, students who encounter this approach as part of the school curriculum are usually required to participate in this group; and they do not escape from the others when the session is over. Whatever happens here will be remembered by the peers they face daily—in math, in history, on the playing field, on the bus home. This is no easy challenge for any of us; it is a delicate process, requiring patience and respect.

A respectful pace and nonintrusive methods honor the mistrust and cynicism teenagers feel about voicing what is really in their hearts. Playful games in the early weeks foster affection, cooperation, and connection in the group. They help students learn as much as possible about others without feeling exposed or invaded. Carefully selected activities invite students slowly, cautiously, playfully to get to know each other.

Each class period, like each semester, has its own rhythm, designed to ease students into and out of a time of sharing honestly about significant teenage issues. A class might begin with a game that brings everyone together quickly through laughter. Or it might open with symbolic expression as students work with a lump of clay or crayons and paper to create a symbol of how they are feeling "right now." A repertoire of warm-up exercises helps students relax, let go of distractions, and interact with one another in a casual way before being asked to speak before the whole group. Unlike programs that begin with "boundary breakers," I have learned that respecting the caution, pace, and privacy of each student is what allows them to tell their stories with authenticity and depth.

After the groundwork is laid, students begin to find the comfort or the courage to begin talking about their own lives. Personal storytelling brings a group to life because it ensures that students speak about what they have experienced and know. It gives speakers a sense of authority over their own lives and begins to develop the listener's capacity for empathy. Through their stories, students reveal what in their lives awakens and feeds their souls.

"Bring in an object that symbolizes something that is really im-portant to you right now in your life," I tell a group of high school seniors in Colorado.

"Does the object have to be valuable?" a student asks.

"No, the object is just a symbol. It could be something you cherish, but it can also be a trivial object that symbolizes something important to you right now."

The students bring their objects in paper bags, so no one will know who brought them. One or two students have forgotten, so I give them crayons and paper to draw their symbol. They all leave the room so I can lay out the objects on a beautiful cloth in the center of the room. When they come back in, no one knows who brought the ring, the book, the cupcake, the exquisitely delicate small box, the stone, the set of keys, the painting, or the locket. One at a time, the students choose an item that intrigues them.

Ryan goes first, picking up the cupcake. "Do I get to eat it, too?" he asks mischievously. Giggles ripple throughout the room. "Who brought this great-looking thing?" He looks around the circle and Karen nods shyly. "What does it mean to you, Karen?" he asks. "What's the story?"

"One of my friends loves this kind of cupcake," Karen explains. "Whenever I know she's down, I go to the one store in town that makes these, and I surprise her with one. I have some very good friends in my life, and those friendships are what's most important to me right now."

Other students, when their objects are chosen, talk about surprising gains and disturbing losses in the lives of their families. One student feels blessed and surprised by a rose given her by her stepgrandparents. The next student tells a more typical tale from the divorce wars.

"This is my Dad's wedding ring," says Jen, holding up a thick gold band. "I wear it now, since they divorced. He travels a lot, and I worry about him. Wearing the ring on a chain around my neck keeps him close to me. And it reminds me of how precious relationships are and how quickly they can be gone."

Petra has brought a picture of her family and laid a cross on top of it—a cross she had made herself, carved out of wood, with a lifesaver glued in the center of the cross.

"I became a Christian a few years back. It's been the most wonderful thing in my life. I can't tell you what it feels like to know that I'm loved like that. Always loved and guided. By Jesus. And it's brought our family much closer."

Tension comes over me as I wonder how the other students will react to religious fervor in the classroom. But what I see in their faces is a relaxed openness, curiosity, respect. Petra, too, reads the room, and her face brightens with a beautiful smile.

"Guys—it's amazing," she concludes.

Because each story comes straight from the heart, these students are quickly engaged, eager to listen. Many of them are surprised to feel respect for classmates they never knew or wanted to know. Many notice more similarities than they expected. The students become calm when they discover how easy it is to enter the circle and be heard.

Working with 8th and 9th grade students in Oakland, California, Folásadé Oládélé (1998/1999) created a similar approach. "As part of encouraging a sense of spirit in the classroom," says Oládélé, "I helped students develop . . . 'sacred symbols' that exposed more of the students' personal aspirations and desires. Every student performed an oral presentation of his or her symbol to applause and support from the entire group" (p. 65). Telling stories about the symbols they bring with them, students introduce themselves to each other through what they value most in life. Whether it is the objects they bring to represent what is most important in their lives or the clay they mold into a symbol of their feelings, symbols allow students to reveal their emotions *indirectly*. Through such exercises, they have the freedom to explore and express feelings that might otherwise be too private or uncomfortable to put into words this early in the semester.

With seniors, I have found we can quickly build an environment safe enough to invite students to share what is meaningful to them. For younger students, our early discussions circle around friendship and the qualities we look for in a friend. We tell stories about childhood—supporting distance before asking students to reveal the more vulnerable experiences and feelings of the present.

Although symbols are a valuable source of inspiration, nothing elicits stories more powerfully than students' own questions. To find out what is on their minds, we do something radical: We ask them.

The Mysteries Questions

> Be patient toward all that is unsolved in your heart and try to love the *questions themselves* like locked rooms and like books that are written in a very foreign tongue. Do not now seek the answers which cannot be given you because you would not be able to live them. And the point is, to live everything. *Live* the questions now. Perhaps you will then gradually, without noticing it, live along some distant day into the answer.
>
> —RAINER MARIA RILKE (1962, p. 35)

At about the fourth or fifth week of the course, when the beginnings of trust emerge, we ask our students to anonymously write their personal mysteries.

"Please write about what you wonder about when you cannot sleep at night," we suggest, "or when you're walking alone to the school bus, or when you're jogging on the track. What do you worry about? or feel curious about? or feel afraid or excited about? What are your questions about yourselves, about others, about life itself?"

We *never* ask students to speak aloud about their private mysteries. Only if this process is completely *anonymous* are students safe. Only then will we hear the truth. If you as the teacher are familiar with students' handwriting, you might give the original papers to a colleague to type before reading them.

The promise of *complete anonymity* in our mysteries questions frees students to have a rare glimpse into the hearts of their peers; they are always surprised and greatly relieved by the common concerns they find there.

Gary Comstock, a professor of leadership development and chaplain at Wesleyan University, also uses anonymous writing to elicit unusual depth and honesty. He gives his students a topic or a question, hands out index cards, and asks them to write anonymously what feels most important to them about the theme. Comstock (personal interview, 1999) believes that "authority never really breaks down" in the classroom, "even if I'm the nicest person in the world. Students still need to express some things with utter safety—not just because of how I'd react but also their peers. There are things people are ready to own and others they must process first before being ready to own."

From the inner city, from small towns, and from affluent suburbs, I have collected thousands of questions from students in 7th through 12th grades. The range is broad, but more impressive are the patterns of yearning and confusion that appear again and again.

Let us listen first to a few "mysteries about myself" from high school seniors:[3]

☙ *Why am I so angry?*

☙ *Why am I so alone?*

☙ *Why do I feel scared and confused about becoming an adult? What does it mean to accept that this is my life and I have responsibility for it?*

---

[3]All questions in italic format are anonymous "mysteries questions" from students in public and private schools across the United States.

❧ *Why am I not pretty like my sister is?*
❧ *How do I know I'm "normal"?*
❧ *What is normal?*

When asked to ponder their mysteries about other people and about life or the universe, seniors ask questions like these:

❧ *Why do people hate others—black, white, Hispanic?*
❧ *Why do people do drugs?*
❧ *Will my brother have the same temper/addictions as my father?*
❧ *Will we ever have a woman or a black president?*
❧ *How do people who love you hurt you? Why?*
❧ *Why do people tire of life?*
❧ *What is our purpose in life?*
❧ *How do I know the world around me is safe, in existence, and not going to end any minute?*

Younger students have already begun this search. In 9th and 10th grade, they chew on questions like these:

❧ *What do people think about me?*
❧ *How does one determine sexuality? Are there symptoms? Is it a decision or a natural given—are you stuck with it or is it a choice?*
❧ *Why can't I trust people who are trustworthy and not trust people who aren't?*
❧ *Why am I so heartless to so many people?*
❧ *Why is it so hard to get along with others at this age? Why? Why? Why?*
❧ *Why have we ruined our earth?*
❧ *I wonder who is God, or if there is God? If there is a God, why is there so much Bad on Earth?*
❧ *Does it hurt to die?*

With questions ranging from the mundane to the profound, 7th and 8th grade students also reveal the challenging dilemmas of adolescence:

❧ *Am I so annoying and so unfriendly that some people ignore, act mean, or talk behind my back—I don't want anyone to hate me.*
❧ *Why do I have to make myself look nice for other people? Why can't I just act like myself and not have to impress anybody?*
❧ *When do I get tall?*
❧ *What is it like to be old?*

≈ *Why don't I always get along with my parents?*

≈ *Why do boys always like stuck-up girls?*

≈ *How do you know if you love a boy or girlfriend? What is a good time to loose [sic] virginity?*

≈ *What happens when you're pressured into sex?*

≈ *Why don't my parents trust me?*

≈ *Why are people so cold in taking care of our planet?*

≈ *How come people kill other people?*

≈ *Where do we go when we die?*

These "mysteries questions" allow us to refine our curriculum to respond personally to each group. By doing so, student concerns become central to the curriculum, not peripheral or irrelevant.

The following week, we read aloud *all* the questions—completely unedited and uncensored. We read them in a ceremonial way with honor and respect. When their questions are read back in their entirety, students are stunned by the depth and wisdom of their peers. They always express relief that they are not alone. This public, respectful witnessing of their personal mysteries is a turning point for each group.

"So now are you going to answer all of them?" a student will often joke. In this humorous way, they reveal their awareness that most of these questions do not call for answers, certainly not by a classroom teacher in a public school.

"If we are to open up the spiritual dimension of education, we must understand that spiritual questions do not have answers in the way math problems do," writes Parker Palmer (1998), one of the first contemporary writers to write about the role of spirituality in education. "Giving one another The Answer is part of what shuts us down. When people ask these deep questions, they do not want to be saved but simply to be heard; they do not want fixes or formulas but compassion and companionship on the demanding journey called life" (p. 8). Palmer also acknowledges that "our real questions are asked largely in our hearts because it is too risky to ask them in front of one another."

As I have tried to understand what encourages the spiritual development of students, anonymous, heartfelt questions have been a vital tool. These questions give us as teachers immediate access to the wonder, worry, curiosity, fear, and excitement that burns inside our students.

The Council Process

On the day we read the mysteries questions aloud, we have our first council. Like the sharing circles we have had earlier in the semester, a council meeting gives each person a chance to speak without immediate reaction or dialogue. But the council shifts the atmosphere by the use of a few simple ritual elements, as follows:

If the student and parent community are comfortable with candles, we begin by lighting candles in the center with a student dedication or two for that day's council:

- "I dedicate this council to honesty—and the friendships that come when we tell the truth."
- "I dedicate this council to my grandpa, who is very sick right now and I'm worried about him."
- "I dedicate this council to our soccer team, which just won the state championship!"

With the lights dimmed, the candles create the intimacy of a campfire. On rare occasions, I have met students for whom the lighting of a candle means the invocation of the devil or evil spirits. If I suspect that such religious beliefs are present, I ask if there are any objections to lighting a candle. If there are any, I will substitute fresh flowers or other objects of natural beauty or invite students to bring something of beauty to put in the center.

The smooth stone we pass to designate who has the right to speak protects each speaker from interruption. A timekeeper with a discreet bell ensures that each student has equal time. Students practice the "deep listening" (Zimmerman & Coyle, 1996) that is central to the council process—listening with complete attention, unimpeded by quick judgments and reactions, hearing the speaker's feelings and intentions, as well as the words. For many students, the elements of simple ritual make our conversation feel more meaningful and safe than ordinary talk.

Throughout the semester, I offer themes that allow students to find out more about one another and about themselves, such as the following:

- *Trust*—a time someone in your life was really there for you; and *mistrust*—a time when someone let you down.
- *A precious moment* from childhood you want never to forget.
- *Childhood fears* you may be still learning to overcome.
- A *decision* you had to make and how you made it.
- *Being left out* or excluding someone else.

Through storytelling about these and other themes, students quickly engage with each other at a new level.

The Map Emerges

When my students described what they had heard about this program from previous students, they often used the word "spiritual." I wanted to know what they meant by that word. Rather than seek a metaphysical definition, I decided to ask them directly. I waited until well into the semester, when a sense of community had begun to form. In my "Senior Passage" course—the program in which Felicia participated—I asked my seniors: "What does spirit mean to you?"

"We've been talking about wholeness in this class—about caring for ourselves as whole people," I begin carefully. "It's pretty clear what we mean by mind and body and even what we mean by social and emotional needs. But what do we mean by spiritual?"

At first they call out words like "religion," "soul," "meditation," "peace," "holy," and "God." It is an important beginning, but I am looking for a way to discover a more personal definition of their spiritual nature.

"Would you be willing to each tell us a story about a time in your lives when your own spirit—whatever that means to you—was nourished?" I ask.

"What do you mean 'nourished'?" they ask.

"You know—encouraged, stimulated, inspired. . . . Whatever comes to mind."

Their eyes take on a dreamy quality as they begin searching. Everybody has a story—a story that commands the full, riveted attention of each student in the room.

Many stories are about nature or about a sense of belonging. Others are about the joy of creativity, the strength that comes through challenge or even suffering, the awe that comes from discovering faith in God.

As I listen to these stories, my heart is moved, and my own spirit is nourished. Finally, I have been willing to ask and they are willing to speak about the spiritual dimension of their lives.

∞ ∞ ∞

After listening for many years to their stories, questions, and wisdom, I began to see a pattern. Certain experiences—quite apart from religious belief or affiliation—had a powerful effect in nourishing the spiritual development of young people. As the pattern became clearer, a map emerged. I found seven gateways to their souls, each gateway representing a set of key experiences embedded in their stories. Together these gateways offer both a language and a framework for developing practical teaching strategies to invite soul into the classroom. Ordinary activities—easily integrated into school life—can have an extraordinary effect in meeting needs long neglected for so many teenagers.

Each gateway begins with a yearning—a yearning that is sometimes fulfilled by merely being acknowledged, a yearning for experiences that can often be fostered in classrooms where the heart is safe and the soul is welcomed. The remaining seven chapters in this book explore these gateways: the yearning for deep connection, the longing for silence and solitude, the search for meaning and purpose, the hunger for joy and delight, the creative drive, the urge for transcendence, and the need for initiation (see Figure 1.1).

Each of these domains can be a gateway to spiritual development, a path for nourishing "the soul of students." They are not, however, a developmental sequence, not stages that each student goes through in a particular order. Some students will be engaged and satisfied through certain gateways and not through others. Often the gateways are not distinct, but overlap and interact for each student, individually.

As we explore each gateway, we will hear the stories of educators, as well as the stories and questions of young people, like Felicia, who have been my primary source in discovering the many paths leading to the soul of students.

FIGURE 1.1

Seven Gateways to the Soul in Education

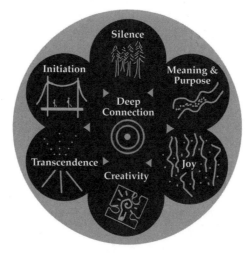

1. The yearning for deep connection describes a quality of relationship that is profoundly caring, is resonant with meaning, and involves feelings of belonging, or of being truly seen and known. Students may experience deep connection to themselves, to others, to nature, or to a higher power.

2. The longing for silence and solitude, often an ambivalent domain, is fraught with both fear and urgent need. As a respite from the tyranny of "busyness" and noise, silence may be a realm of reflection, of calm or fertile chaos, an avenue of stillness and rest for some, prayer or contemplation for others.

3. The search for meaning and purpose concerns the exploration of big questions, such as "Why am I here?" "Does my life have a purpose? How do I find out what it is?" "What is life for?" "What is my destiny?" "What does my future hold?" and "Is there a God?"

4. The hunger for joy and delight can be satisfied through experiences of great simplicity, such as play, celebration, or gratitude. It also describes the exaltation students feel when encountering beauty, power, grace, brilliance, love, or the sheer joy of being alive.

5. The creative drive, perhaps the most familiar domain for nourishing the spirit in school, is part of all the gateways. Whether developing a new idea, a work of art, a scientific discovery, or an entirely new lens on life, students feel the awe and mystery of creating.

6. The urge for transcendence describes the desire of young people to go beyond their perceived limits. It includes not only the mystical realm, but experiences of the extraordinary in the arts, athletics, academics, or human relations. By naming and honoring this universal human need, educators can help students constructively channel this powerful urge.

7. The need for initiation deals with rites of passage for the young—guiding adolescents to become more conscious about the irrevocable transition from childhood to adulthood. Adults can give young people tools for dealing with all of life's transitions and farewells. Meeting this need for initiation often involves ceremonies with parents and faculty that welcome them into the community of adults.

2

Deep Connection

❧ *Sometimes I think about how many good friends I have, and it doesn't seem like I have very many.*

❧ *Why do I have such a hard time letting people get close to me—especially those of the opposite sex?*

❧ *Why does my Mom hate me?*

❧ *I want to know if I'll ever have a relationship with my Dad.*

What is the quality of relationships that nourish the soul of students? Whether it is a relationship to one's own self, to others, or to the world, the experience of deep connection arises when there is a profound respect, a deep caring, and a quality of "being with" that honors the truth of each participant in the relationship. Young people are crying out to be seen and heard so that they, in turn, can take in the world through learning, loving, and serving. Students who feel deeply connected through at least one such relationship are more likely to survive the "lure of risk" (Elias et al., 1997) and the damage of stress; they are more likely to discover and contribute the gift they are meant to bring to the world. "Spirituality is nourished, not through formal rituals that students practice in school," says holistic educator Ron Miller (1995), "but by the *quality of relationship* that is developed between person and world" (p. 5).

As students tell their stories about when their spirit was nourished, many are infused with this quality of deep connection. Whether it is the young people in Felicia's group connecting deeply to each other in both celebration and grief, or Karen talking about the cupcakes she brought her friend; whether it is Jen marking the pain of her parents' divorce through the cast-off wedding ring now worn around her neck, or Petra connecting deeply to Jesus through her faith, the moments of deep connection in the lives of young people are resonant with caring and with soul.

Young people who thrive have encountered deep connection. They feel they belong—that people know them. Suffering and violence trail the lives of those who are without such connections. A recent article on youth suicide captures the power of authentic connection in promoting spiritual and psychological resilience (Ward, 1996). In his diary, a young man "who ultimately did not survive the tortured isolation of his youth," had an inkling of what might have prevented his death. He wrote:

> All I know is that the few times I have truly touched and been touched by another person—those few times when I have really seen, and likewise been acknowledged as a reality and not a projection—the reward, the pure exhilarating freshness, was unmistakable (p. 35).

For this young man, unfortunately, such experiences were rare indeed. Students who thrive have had parents or teachers who have provided a wealth of opportunities for deep connection.

Several aspects of deep connection have emerged from my students' stories—connection to the self, to one other person or an authentic community, to lineage, nature, or a higher power. Let's look at each theme to gain a practical understanding of deep connection and learn how we can foster experiences that open this gateway.

Deep Connection to the Self

✎ *Why do I go through mood swings? Why do they lead me into depression?*

✎ *What, of all I feel and believe, is truly my own? Is there anything left beyond that which others have implanted within me?*

✎ *Do I try to please others more than myself?*

✎ *How can I change feeling lonely?*

✎ *How can I know the difference between selfishness and being fair to myself?*

The capacity to be in relationship to one's inner life is critical for the development of autonomy—building a healthy identity that is central to adolescent development. In the research on resilience in young people, authors often refer to autonomy as a "need," "social value," "capacity," or "strength" (Brendtro, Brokenleg, & Van Bockern, 1990). Here, as in other aspects of deep connection, spiritual development is interwoven with healthy emotional or psychological development.

Although young people are filled with questions about themselves, much of modern life keeps them from the search to understand and care for themselves. Television, video games, and now the Internet are all pulling adolescents into almost addictive outer-directedness. The natural urge to "belong" may also be so strong during this lonely age that social life takes priority over self-discovery.

Moments of deep connection to the self—when we really know ourselves, express our true self, feel connected to the essence of who we are—nourish the human spirit. Some people define this connection to the self as the bedrock of spirituality, from which all other connections flow. "I find my spirit when I'm all alone, and I have to look at myself deep down inside," says one high school senior in Oregon.

Experiences of deep connection to the self may come in the midst of other people but are more likely to occur in times of solitude. "I like to take time to go within myself sometimes," says Katrina. "And when I do that, I try to take an emptiness inside there. I think that everyone struggles to find their own way with their spirit, and it's in the struggle that our spirit comes forth."

Through being alone, we can contact the deeper truth of our natures. Once we are profoundly honest with ourselves, we may see reality (and other people) with greater objectivity and openness.

Deep Connection to Another

∞ *Will I ever find true love?*

∞ *Is there anyone out in the world like me?*

∞ *How do people who love you hurt you? Why?*

∞ *Why don't parents understand that the children of a divorce have to go on loving both parents?*

∞ *Why is intimacy only sexual?*

∞ *I sometimes go against one or two of my values just to be accepted, and I don't know why I do that.*

Authentic intimacy—a deeply caring, mutual, respectful relationship with one other person—can be a source of deep connection for young people. The stories they tell are usually about close connections with a friend, mentor, or parent, rather than romantic forms of intimacy. Many students talk about discovering a new friend, to whom they could tell everything:

> When I invited Jane over for a sleepover, we had only hung out a
> couple of times. Once we started to talk, we couldn't stop. It was
> like meeting my twin! We had so much in common—the way we
> think, feel, even some of the ways we describe things. I had never
> felt so connected to someone before—I didn't know that feeling
> was possible. That feeling—when you just can't believe how
> close you feel to a stranger—that's what feeds my spirit.

Although students rarely talk about it, I believe that when young
people seek intimacy through sexual relationships, or even having a
baby, they are trying to nourish this spiritual yearning for deep connection. Of course, teenagers rarely find the genuine intimacy they are
looking for down these pathways. The pressures and confusions of sexual activity in a teen relationship often undermine or destroy the growing intimacy. Most teenagers have little ego strength and a poorly
developed sense of autonomy, self-knowledge, and personal boundaries. Thus they are extremely ambivalent about the authenticity and
surrender required to experience intimacy with a romantic partner.
Providing opportunities for authentic, age-appropriate intimacy may
well ease the desperation that leads many teenagers to premature sexuality.

For some students, a rich and meaningful friendship does arise in
the context of romance, which provides a genuine experience of deep
connection. "When I go to the grave site, I get this very special feeling,"
said a junior on the lower east side of Manhattan in her "family group"
class. "I was so close to my boyfriend before he got shot. It wasn't just
romance—we were best friends. I still feel that closeness, when I'm
with him at his grave."

Mia, a senior in Colorado, mused:

> I wonder if everybody's truth is different. My faith, my truth, is
> love and true companionship. I believe I have found my soul
> mate; and to me, that is the meaning of life, that connection. I
> don't think that is true for everybody, though.

The powerful drive to individuate can strain the closeness some
students have had for years with parents. When this deep connection
diminishes during the teenage years, parents may feel confused or
hurt, or even a profound sense of loss. Parents who honor this distance
during the teenage years (without pulling away themselves) often are
rewarded by a return of even deeper closeness once the young person
feels that he is standing more firmly on his own.

I have seen some seniors become really close to a parent—sometimes for the first time—after stepping out into an independence that

makes them feel secure in the integrity of their new self. Kelly brought many students to tears in a senior passage class, when she talked about the object that symbolized what was really important to her in her life:

> This raggedy old doll belonged to my Mom, and she gave it to me. My mother and I have gotten really close this year, and we never were before. But it's bittersweet, because it's gonna be really difficult to leave.

Some students have had the rare opportunity to connect deeply to other adults—a relative, a teacher, or even a stranger who becomes a mentor committed to guiding this young person in a personal way. Profound nourishment of soul can occur when young people feel a significant bond with an adult who actively chooses to share precious time and wisdom.

Deep Connection to Community

∞ *Why am I so alone? Why do I feel like the burden of the world is on my shoulders?*

∞ *What is the thread of humanity that connects all of us?*

∞ *Why are there so many cruel people?*

∞ *How can I let people know what I feel, when I don't trust hardly anyone?*

∞ *Why is it that people rarely look past the outer shell (mental and physical) of a person?*

The yearning to connect meaningfully with a group or community is strong in teenagers. A *meaningful* connection includes respect and care that encourages authenticity for each individual in the group. Such a group encourages young people to reveal more and more of their own selves, knowing that others will see and hear them for who they really are. Such acceptance creates a deep connection with community that leads to a sense of belonging.

Some people see "belonging," like autonomy, as a spiritual need that overlaps with a basic psychological need. "The spiritual hunger," writes J. G. Bennett (1984) in *The Spiritual Hunger of the Modern Child,* ". . . starts really with this necessity for us to 'belong,' to have a place, to feel that we are not isolated, that there is something beyond our own psyche which is not a stranger to us, which is not outside of us" (p. 4).

Authors often cite "belonging" in the literature on resilience in youth: Students who feel a sense of belonging are loving, friendly, cooperative, and able to trust and form healthy attachments. The consequences for teenagers who have not been given opportunities for genuine belonging are disastrous. Several educators (Brendtro et al., 1990) who have specialized in working with severely alienated youth observe that

> some youth who feel rejected are struggling to find artificial, distorted belongings through behavior such as attention seeking or running with gangs. Others have abandoned the pursuit and are reluctant to form human attachments. In either case, their unmet needs can be addressed by corrective relationships of trust and intimacy (p. 47).

The move to community-building in education—through the middle school reform movement, social and emotional learning, and holistic education—reflects a growing awareness of the profound need of children and adolescents to feel a part of something larger than themselves and their families. Especially for adolescents, meeting the yearning to belong becomes all the more urgent when the ties to community outside of school have been frayed and broken for many students.

To feel a sense of belonging at school, students must be part of a community in the classroom where they feel seen and heard for who they really are. Many teachers regularly create this opportunity through "morning meetings," a weekly opportunity for "council," or other forms of "sharing circles" offered with ground rules that make it safe to be vulnerable.

"I feel this bond with all of you," said Peter to the others in his geology class, which included a "senior passage" component. "I've never felt this way in a group before." Peter continued, "I guess that's what I think of when I think about spirit."

Such authentic expression can emerge only in a climate of safety, caring, and respect. "It is in close, ongoing, meaningful groups when students are likely to feel spiritual connections to others," write Weaver and Cotrell (1992) about their experience of nurturing spirit at the college level.

> It is through such *cooperation* (working together in groups), *companionship* (coming together as friends), *compassion* (revealing sympathetic concern for others and a desire to help them), and *communion* (moments when we let go of preconceived ideas about each other and communicate as openly and authentically as we can), that spirituality is nurtured in the classroom (James & James, cited in Weaver & Cotrell, 1992, p. 433, emphasis added).

The first two stages—*cooperation* and *companionship*—are well accepted as crucial capacities in social competence in most educational settings. *Compassion* and *communion,* however, are where the emotional and social realm merges with the spiritual.

As caring companions and elders truly hear and see students—in their wisdom and confusion, their pain and their joy—the students take a dramatic leap in developing resilience and maturity. And when teachers invite parents into the classroom to share with their children in this climate of deep respect and caring, even more possibilities emerge in schools for fulfilling the human spirit.

If group experiences are to have this beneficial effect, school leaders must be as supportive to the autonomy of the individual as they are to fostering a sense of belonging and union with the group. Autonomy and intimacy—these needs may appear to be contradictory, but they are not. *The more we encourage young people to strengthen their own boundaries and develop their own identity, the more capable they are of bonding to a group in a healthy, enduring way.*

When a classroom becomes safe for each individual and point of view, students begin to reveal fundamental differences of opinion, values, and beliefs. This can take a long time with some of today's youth who are broken, disruptive, and fearful of feelings. If a group can reach a stage of genuine intimacy, airing their differences allows students to develop an open mind and a broader perspective essential in our highly diverse society. It was in a group of 15-year-olds in California that I first witnessed this.

The outbreak of the Gulf War is a deeply troubling moment for our school. Parents of high school seniors are worried about their boys being taken. Students, teachers, and parents alike are struggling with the moral and political dilemmas of going to war. I am teaching at a progressive high school, and many of the faculty are veterans of '60s "teach-ins." We decide to hold a teach-in that week to examine the issues in Kuwait.

The next day, in my 10th grade class, I suspend my lesson plans, so my students can discuss their feelings about the war. After Mikaela expresses her opposition to the war, her voice begins to waver: "You know that student from Kuwait who spoke yesterday? He was so sad, so scared. His family is in such danger! Such terrible things are happening to his people. And when he told us what was real for him and for his people, our students jeered and booed him!" She begins to cry.

"Can you believe they did that?" She looks earnestly around the circle again. "Can you believe they would do that? How could they? He's a human being, with real feelings and beliefs. I don't happen to agree with his beliefs, either. But how can we do that to each other? Just because we don't agree, how can we treat each other that way?"

In that silent, tear-filled moment, Mikaela challenged us to see how easily our humanity is eroded when politics becomes more important than people. The students who followed spoke passionately and were often polarized, yet the group listened to each with great interest and compassion. I had never before seen such a hot political issue explored with such mutual respect between adversaries—not among teenagers and not even among adults. Through encounters with deep differences *in a compassionate context,* many students begin to grasp both the immense possibilities for human connection and the tragic hold of hostile separation.

"When we are touched by people with whom we do not agree, we begin to believe in the possibility of nonviolent resolution of conflicts," writes Nel Noddings (1992). "At the same time, when we recognize the reality of hate in opposing parties, and our love for both helps us to understand their hatred, we begin to understand a basic tragedy of human life" (p. 57).

Such experiences are an antidote to the alienation and isolation of youth, or to the desperate search for belonging in dangerous settings such as cults and gangs. As teenagers pull away from their parents to form an independent identity, the values and opinions of their peers naturally become more important. When schools create the conditions for soulful communication between students and with caring adults, adolescents are less likely to fall prey to the damaging and potentially life-threatening "belonging" of the streets and drug cultures.

For students who have had the opportunity to participate in meaningful groups, the experience of communion may become an ongoing part of life. When students regularly experience (during the school year) how it feels to have another person or a group truly see and hear them, they may develop the capacities and the faith required for them to create these experiences throughout their lives.

Deep Connection to Lineage

❧ *Does my heritage mean anything in who I am?*
❧ *Who are our ancestors—the real ancestors? How did they act? What is so different from us?*

For some students, an encounter with their roots—with the ancient place of their people or with particular ancestors who influenced their lives—can begin to nourish their spirit:

> You see, really my name came from my great great-grandmother
> who died in the Holocaust. When she died, her daughter, a child

at the time, named herself Sarah—she changed her name. That child was my mother's grandmother–really close to my mother. When she died, and I was born, my mother named me Sarah. Sometimes it almost seems like Sarah's such a common name that it's not a good name to have. But when I think about where it comes from, it's a lot deeper than the five letters.

Discovering the power of lineage as a call to the soul, I looked for lessons that could take my students into this realm. I ask them to bring us a story about both their first and last names. Where did these names come from? How was their name chosen? Does it have a particular meaning? How do they feel about their name?

When we gather for this lesson, I begin with the story of my name. They are surprised that a single name can carry so much history. Immigration, assimilation, feminism, anti-Semitism, World War II—powerful forces in the American story are evoked within the story of my name. It inspires my students to look deeply into the strands of connection and meaning that flow from their own names. As they each tell their own story, we weave a tapestry rich with the many colors and textures of American life.

James has a somber, downcast look as he comments on his name:

My first name comes from my father, and his father, and probably his father before him. But our last name— Walker—well, that's a slave name. I mean, some slave owner probably gave my people that name. I have no way to know what our real name was.

Many teachers use family names as a way to encourage students to connect to their lineage and to their own wisdom traditions. "I asked students to write down the name of an ancestor or someone they loved and who loved them and wished the best for them," writes Folásedé Oládélé (1998/1999). "Whenever they had doubts about whether they were meeting the highest standards in their behavior or in their assignments, they reflected on what this person might say" (p. 65).

Others, like 8th grade English teacher Colleen Conrad, invite students to explore their roots in writing autobiographies:

I had a student named Oran whose family had fled Mongolia during a time of religious persecution. She missed her homeland terribly, and she wrote an incredibly beautiful tribute to her grandmother. She described the hut where her grandmother lived and where she had often stayed—what it was like to herd sheep on the hillsides and the stories her grandmother would share with her in the evenings after they'd worked together all day. She knew she would never see her grandmother again (interview, 1999).

People who know something about their family history often experience great power in their sense of lineage. Connecting to the people and the land from which we come can embed us in a chain of continuity that deeply stirs the soul.

But many of our students have no knowledge of their ancestry. As they listen to peers or teachers who draw strength from that ancient pool, a yearning rises in those who have previously been unaware of how lineage can bring a larger, more enduring frame of belonging.

To support students who have no viable connection to their own ancestry, we invite them to address this question: "Who has been an elder to you—whether you have blood ties or not?" One student, George, responds as he struggles to decide if he had a story to tell about ancestors or elders:

> For me, I'd have to say that James's mother–Stella–has been my elder. She took me in as one of her own—there was no distinction. Even though I was Hispanic and they were African American, she showed no difference in how she treated me from how she treated her children. She was always loving, but she was tough. Stella civilized me from being basically a wild animal. My family had no rules, no discipline, no structure. She really gave that to me.

> Before I met that family, I used to feel sometimes that nature was my mother. I would go out and sit for a long time and talk to nature and get answers to my question. Sometimes I would just lie on a rock and feel the love coming from that rock. I know it sounds silly, but I believe you can have a relationship with a rock.

In an interview, Conrad (1999) describes another student "who came from a mixed family. Her father was Hispanic and her mother was white. Jasmine's parents were divorced, and her mother was reluctant to give Jasmine much exposure to her Hispanic heritage. Jasmine was consumed with the desire to know more about her roots and her father's family. She wrote and wrote about not being allowed to know one's heritage and how that gave a person no foundation. The writing seemed to help her sort through her feelings."

Students long for a sense of connection to something larger and more enduring than friends or family. Connecting to their own people or place—or even to an elder who takes them into a strong sense of traditional ways that are not their own—can give them the faith and perspective that can make their daily fears, losses, and failures more bearable and more meaningful. Teachers have also discovered the spiritual dimension in connecting to their own lineage:

> I took a trip, about two years ago, to Scotland, where my people come from. I had never been there, and I wanted to trace my family's history. I went back to this little town where I knew they had lived, and I met an old man who had known some of my ancestors. He was happy to show me around. He took me to these houses—shacks, really—where different relatives had lived. And he told me stories—what was known about these people.
>
> After visiting the town, he took me on a walk just outside of town, up a steep hill, a little mountain actually. Everything was so green. We kept walking up and then he stopped and beckoned me to turn around. I looked down on the valley below—I could see the whole village.
>
> I looked down and I felt . . . [she hesitates, looking for the word] connected. I felt so connected. To the land, the people, the village, my history. [Her face is flushed with feeling.]
>
> I had never felt that way before. It was so strong. So unexpected. So wonderful. I guess you could say it was a spiritual experience.

This teacher had been teaching social and emotional learning for years—yet, until that moment, she had not considered that her work might have an effect on the soul of students. Through her own deep connection to the land of her people, Cara began to understand that she could safely welcome soul into her classroom.

Deep Connection to Nature

– *How can people see God's fingerprints and not believe he touched nature?*

– *How come we as people see nature as so spiritual yet constantly destroy it?*

– *Will the environment survive for my children and their children?*

– *People all over the world look at the same night sky, the same stars and moon and it always appears to be right above you no matter where you are.*

– *How can nature somehow always be beautiful even when everything else in life is terribly ugly?*

Although endangered nature can be a source of fear and anxiety for young people, those who have discovered a deep connection with the natural world also find a great source of comfort and joy. Whether it is with a tree in a small urban park or on a journey far away from the man-made world, young people often discover in nature an experience of peace, gratitude, or belonging to something larger and more meaningful than day-to-day existence.

"When I get depressed," revealed Keisha to her "family group" members in a school in Manhattan, "I go to this park near my house where there is an absolutely enormous tree. I go and sit down with it because it feels so strong to me."

Other students have had the privilege of going into the wild. "I went on Outward Bound last summer. It was a turning point," said Lorraine in a Passages class in Boulder. "The group experience was important, my personal challenges were awesome. But what really changed me was seeing how charged I get just being in the wilderness. The beauty, the majesty—it's indescribable, the power I feel inside when I'm deep in the forest or walking along a rushing river."

"I was out fishing in a boat on a lake and caught a fish," said Will in Oregon. "I admired its beauty and power and then I released it. I let go of my power over it. At that moment, I felt connected to spirit."

One girl, who lived with a chronically depressed mother, told the story of a camping trip with her father, whom she rarely saw. "We lived by the natural rhythms of nature, rising with the sun and going to sleep at dark. That's what I loved." Her story went on to weave the joy of connecting deeply to nature with connecting to her father.

For some, it is the beauty and majesty of nature that calls forth awe or wonder that satisfies the spirit. For others, it is the power and mystery, which defies human control and puts everyday problems or disappointments into perspective. The rhythms of nature, the eternal cycles of the day and the seasons, give some students a sense of participation in a larger frame of meaning. The experience of space and freedom afforded by a natural setting also gives students at puberty an arena big enough for energies that can be disturbing in the constant confinement of school and home. And for some students, particularly during the middle school years, a natural environment allows them to demonstrate skills and leadership that would never surface in an urban setting:

The last activity on this 7th grade field trip today is our biggest challenge. We have to get each member of the class across "the acid swamp" by swinging them on a rope in such a way that no one's feet touch the ground—or we have to start over. It's a fairly large distance—nothing for young, lithe bodies. But with my middle-aged body, I am afraid I might ruin it for the group.

I have worked long enough with teenagers to realize my fear is an asset. There's no need to hide what I feel by trying to appear "professional."

"I think I could wreck this one for us," I say to the group. "I don't think I can get up the momentum to get myself across before my arms give out."

Sheldon speaks up immediately. We have already noticed his initiative in almost everything we have done that morning. He is not only strong and agile but is a genius for inventing strategies for mastering physical challenges. After being the self-conscious outsider in the verbal activities of our group back at school, Sheldon is emerging as a leader in the wilderness.

"I'll help you, teacher, if you'll let me." Sheldon has a hard time calling me by my name. "I'll do it with you—I'll give you the push you need to get just the right momentum so you can get across but don't boomerang back."

I look at this little guy, and suddenly I see a hero.

"Let's do it," I say with the return of confidence in my voice.

When Sheldon got me across that "dangerous" swamp, he not only saved me and the group from disaster but built a bridge of trust and affection between us that neither of us could muster at school. He was proud—even before the feedback session at the end of the day, when many people showered him with praise and gratitude for his leadership. And having excelled in an element far more inspiring to him than school, Sheldon became an engaged member of our group for the rest of the term.

Nature can change the power balance dramatically in a group of students in a way that shakes things up for the better. Sometimes, the "strong" get weaker and the "weak" get stronger. In the classroom, strength and leadership are usually associated with verbal skills. The kinesthetic stars don't often have a chance to shine. But when we take them all out into nature, the verbally adept often expose their vulnerability; and the group can recognize others for their unique talents. Field trips, orientation programs for new students, and social and emotional learning programs are common ways to take students into nature for after-school, day-long, or overnight field trips.

In my first experience of leading a retreat for high school seniors, I had planned a variety of rich activities for each day. I was confused when my partner, a seasoned outdoor leader, told me I was keeping them too busy and needed to "let the land teach them." What could she mean—let the land teach them? It made no sense to me at the time. But because of my respect for her, I dropped several activities, creating empty spaces in the curriculum. As the days passed, I began to hear in their stories and watch in their faces the teachings of nature. After a brief "solo" time, Alice spoke in council:

As I sat high up on that point overlooking the whole valley, I made my decision. I know which college I'm going to choose, and it feels right. It's been so hard coming to that decision back home; I don't know why. But with all this space around me, it just became clear.

But you know what else I felt? As I looked up to the mountain behind me and down to that huge, beautiful valley, I knew that if I had made the "wrong" decision, if it turned out that a year or two from now, I realized I needed to be somewhere else, that could be okay. It wouldn't be such a disaster, you know. I mean, up till now, I've been feeling like this decision is so big, so important, the most important so far in my life and I've been scared to make it because it seemed so final.

Up on the mountain, nothing in my life seems quite so big any more. Nothing really is so final.

Years later, I hit an unexpected obstacle when I brought my enthusiasm for nature to a school in the Bronx:

I had been working with the teachers all year, helping them start their Senior Passage Course. It had been a rich experience, and now they are enthusiastically planning the spring retreat. Financial limitations permitted only a two-day trip, so we were carefully designing a series of activities that could evoke at least the symbolic essence of a rite of passage.

One teacher, Marion, surprises me by saying, "Our kids just won't show up at the bus if they hear we're spending the night out. They have grown up on the streets. Sure, there's a lot to be afraid of here, but it's a known quantity. They've learned to cope with that fear. But this world hasn't given them a whole lot of trust in life. Nature is totally unknown to them, and it's just too big a risk."

Marion says, "But if we could find a place close enough that would still give them a taste of beauty and nature, we could go early in the morning and come back late at night. Do you think we could design something for a one-day program?"

"Well, let's do it," I say. "We'll just have to see how it works out. I mean, it's either one day or nothing, right?"

They all nod their heads.

Three weeks later, Marion called:

"It was amazing! Incredible! You can't imagine how powerful it was! For the kids, and even more so for some of the faculty who had never seen one of our classes and came along to get a taste of 'Passages.' They were blown away. The land at the retreat center was so beautiful. The kids had a long solo time, moving through a course built into the land for reflection on different life issues. It was perfect! The way they spoke about the silence and the beauty that night at the campfire—everyone was moved. And the stars—these kids had never seen stars like we saw that night. We were all so proud."

I had gone from a five-day retreat in California, to a three-day retreat with my students in Colorado, and now saw that even one day in nature could allow students and teachers to have a peak experience that nourishes spirit.

Deep Connection to a Higher Power

⚭ *How can there be so many religions, and still so many people who don't believe in any religion at all?*

⚭ *Is there life after death?*

⚭ *How did life start?*

⚭ *Is there a God?*

⚭ *What makes people evil?*

Many teenagers wonder whether there is a higher source of power and meaning in the universe to rely on or relate to. For some students, it is precisely their religious faith and experience that is most nourishing to their spirit. But students rarely talk about this in school. Perhaps students perceive fear or hostility when anyone expresses religious views in a school setting. Students for whom a relationship with a higher power is paramount rarely feel safe expressing such feelings in school.

But when students know there is a time in school life to give voice to the comfort and joy they find in religion and in their relationship to God, this freedom of expression is itself nourishing to their spirits. When students with strong religious beliefs have an opportunity to speak to a respectful group of primarily nonbelieving peers about the role of faith in their lives, these devout youth subsequently display a great deal more confidence and leadership in the group. They feel empowered because other people have acknowledged and respected such an important part of their lives.

For many years, I was uncomfortable when students began to talk about God in the classroom. Like most teachers, I was afraid I might be violating the law by allowing these feelings and beliefs into the classroom. I was also afraid that other, nonreligious students might be offended or become anxious about what was going on.

My feelings changed significantly one year when I attended a seminar taught by Charles Haynes and Oliver Thomas at the First Amendment Center at Vanderbilt University. I not only learned more about what the U.S. Constitution permitted, but I also had the opportunity to work together with educators from traditionalist religious groups who have felt profoundly unheard and disempowered by the American schools. We who had been "enemies" according to our ideologies became respectful colleagues together—and even friends. I was deeply moved by my experience in Nashville and came home with my heart open to devout Christians in a new way.

Was it a coincidence that when my new group of seniors brought in their personal symbols to introduce themselves, two girls spoke with eloquence and even zeal about the central importance in their lives of their Christian faith? Each had brought a cross—one hand made and the other an elegant wood carving that had been a gift from her family.

Because the group responded with such comfort to this first offering, these girls shared with ease their relationship to Jesus whenever it felt relevant to them as our class unfolded. In our council on spirit, Debra explained, "I know my spirit is touched when I stop asking for things when I pray to God. When I just pray for nothing."

Allowing such students to share this dimension of their lives, or acknowledging that these students may want to use the times of structured silence or relaxation to engage in private prayer, are expressions of respect for diversity. In no way should they be construed as "teaching religion." For some students, religious experience or a sense of union with God or other representations of a higher power are indeed the most important avenue of spiritual development. We can let them say so while still honoring the First Amendment's provision for separation of church and state. To exclude such an important part of students' lives from discourse in a diverse, authentic classroom community is simply unnecessary.

For some students, it is not God but something mysterious and indescribable that provides a link to a higher source of power or meaning. "My spirit is like some force," said Keith, during a council on nourishing the human spirit. "You know, it's like the excitable ball inside that character in the movie TRON—moving around inside him unpredictably. Spirit is a mystery to me. I don't feel quite comfortable with the word *God*."

The rituals and traditions of Ava's family brought a glow to her face when she spoke one week of her Buddhist name—"which means compassion"—or passed around her medallion the day we shared symbols of what was most important in our lives. "I try to practice being present—that's what Buddhism has given to me that I really cherish. It's the most important thing to me now."

Other students feel something is missing when they listen to peers who are supported by such connection to a higher power. "My parents are independent thinkers," said Sarah after listening to several students who shared the strength and joy that grew out of their relationship to God. "They brought me up without any religion," she lamented. "They never wanted me exposed to that kind of thing. It's hard for me sometimes when I hear some of you guys talk about your relationship to God. I feel like I just don't measure up."

Her voice choked up. "I wonder sometimes about my morals. I'm not sure I really know what spirit is."

Sarah's vulnerability seemed to open something up for this group of seniors working with science teacher Doug Eaton (personal communication, 1999) in Oregon. Later, Liz spoke, looking over at Sarah: "My parents are actually quite religious. They made a great effort to bring me up in their faith. But I couldn't buy in. I just couldn't accept what they were trying to teach me. So I'm finding that I have to work it out myself, too. It's not easy."

Some people ask, "What if their higher power is Satan or other destructive sources of connection—such as cults?" In all my years of teaching, I have never met a student who avowed Satanism or something similar. If it came up, I would speak my heart. While I rarely speak judgmentally to my students, there are times when my integrity and concern for their well-being call me to speak. When one 7th grader praised Hitler and lamented his demise, or when an 8th grader called someone a "faggot" without understanding the layers of cruelty in his comment, I spoke immediately, explaining why I was so disturbed and setting a firm boundary on words and views that violate others.

Whether adolescents feel united with God or feel infused with an ineffable power that transcends humankind and our capacity to know the ultimate workings of the universe, such young people have discovered—in deep connection to a higher power—a source of meaning and faith. Not all students feel the need or the capacity for this aspect of deep connection, but I believe all students benefit from an opportunity to hear from their peers the variety of experiences that human beings discover in the search for spiritual fulfillment.

❧ ❧ ❧

Students who feel deeply connected don't need danger to feel fully alive. They don't need guns to feel powerful. They don't want to hurt others or themselves. Out of connection grow both compassion and passion—for people, for students' goals and dreams, for life itself.

3 *Silence and Stillness*

We hiked through the snow up a mountain ridge and sat on a cliff. An airplane flew over, and the noise from its engines pierced the air. I suddenly thought how noisy the city is back home—but I'm so preoccupied and caught up in my life, that hundreds of airplanes pass over daily and I hardly notice. The contrast makes me appreciate even more this place, this time away.

We listened to the silence. We could hear birds chirping so clearly that we could identify the three pitches of their song. The silence and the view—a snow-capped peak, a valley of green and trees. The mist that covered the peak broke, and revealed the heavens that God alone could have created.

—KALEY WARNER, Colorado senior

It is no coincidence that most of the world's religions have devised a "rest note" into the symphony of the human day, week, or year. Practices such as prayer, meditation, spiritual retreats, Quaker meeting, and the tradition of the Sabbath—all cultivate the capacity for tolerating stillness and create the spaciousness for soul. Brief periods of silence and solitude in school can also give students a tool for cultivating rest and renewal—rest for the nervous system, the mind, the body—which traditional cultures provided routinely. For many of our students and their families, solitude has become a lost art.

We could view silence as a vehicle to go through other gateways: deep connection to the self, transcendence, creative expression, or the search for meaning and purpose. But silence itself can nourish the human spirit, and we should explore its value as a separate gateway.

Rest and Renewal

∾ How can I create the peace within me that will contribute to peace in the Universe?

When we consider offering the opportunity for stillness to our students, we confront a paradox. In many students, we touch the timeless longing of human beings for silence. But we may also contend with a contemporary cultural hostility to this dimension. Silence, stillness, and solitude have been almost eliminated from the lives of children and from U.S. culture in general. A 5th grade student in rural Mississippi writes this essay called "Noise":

> If I were asleep and I had a dream a bad dream and I was just tossing turning and screaming and your dream was about noise in the classroom you can hear pencil sharpeners, pencils beating on the desk feet stumping teachers screaming saying "shut up" you can hear children screaming in the hall beating up against the snack machine you can hear teachers talking to the kids in the room then when you go home in the evening you hear noise and then when you go to school for real your dream comes true you can hear dogs barking garbage trucks picking up garbage bags when you go to the store it not silence it noise because you can hear people the cashers talking and cash registers everywhere you go theres noise.[1]

Noise, speed, and unceasing interaction define modern life for most children. Overstimulation becomes the norm for the child's nervous system. "When I started teaching in the '70s, I'd never heard terms like *tactile defensiveness*," says kindergarten teacher Chris Gerzon in Lexington, Massachusetts. "Now every year I have more kids who have to go work with the occupational therapist because their systems are so overloaded, so overstimulated. Sometimes they wrap them in blankets, just like we used to swaddle our babies to create that sense of stillness and security" (interview, 1999).

"Soul cannot thrive in a fast-paced life," writes Thomas Moore (1992, p. 286) in *Care of the Soul*, "because being affected, taking things in and chewing on them, requires time" (see also Wood, 1999). But slowing down is so foreign to our children that it may be frightening. The constant chatter of television and boom boxes; the never-ending,

---

[1] I am indebted to this child's teacher for evoking and preserving this poem. This young teacher, who gave two years of his life to serve in the severely underresourced schools of the Mississippi Delta is my eldest son, Shane Gerzon-Kessler.

programmed activities of the "hurried child" (Elkind, 1981); the necessity to put children in long hours of group care from early ages—in all these ways children are so underexposed to silence and solitude that some have come to be afraid of any experience of emptiness. So should we speak of a "hunger for silence" when some students are actually repulsed by it?

Every student group I have worked with—from kindergarten through the 12th grade—has had a few students who become agitated by periods of silence. But most settle quickly into the silence. A calm descends on the room—a rest for the nervous system, a respite from the demands of others, and a chance to visit one's own inner life.

Most hover in a state of reflection between waking and sleeping. When they emerge, alertness, freshness, and calmness characterize the group. This change has led me at times, particularly with middle school students, to feel that I am now working with a "different population" than any of my colleagues who share these same students.

Some students go directly to sleep. Many educators think of sleep, like play, as the opposite of work and learning; they banish it from school once students are too old for "naptime." But we don't need to shame our students for falling asleep: Adolescents are often sleep deprived and exhausted. A few moments of sleep can refresh them for hours. "You may have no choice but to fall asleep, and that's all right," I say warmly when we are about to enter the silence. "But if you snore and disrupt other's chance for silence, I will come and put a firm hand on your shoulder to wake you up."

Chip Wood (interview, 1999), one of the founders of "The Responsive Classroom"[2] model, discovered the value of rest and silence early in his career as an educator:

> When I was teaching in public school—I was a principal of a K–8 school in Massachusetts, as well as teaching there full time—I began to look at the middle of the day. Kids would come in from the playground all upset; the lunchroom was a mess; our teachers, like those everywhere, were spending the first 15 minutes after lunch solving recess problems.
>
> I began to think about my experience working in summer camps: You played hard in the morning, then you ate, then you rested. Why not try it in school? So we offered recess first, and then lunch, followed by some quiet time. The children worked

---

[2]The "Responsive Classroom" teaching approach was developed by the Northeast Foundation for Children, 71 Montague City Rd., Greenfield, MA 01301.

up an appetite through play; and then once they got their food in front of them, they would forget those social problems from recess.

The rule for quiet time was that for a half hour, students could do anything that worked for them except speak to someone; they could read, draw, do homework, sleep—"whatever is meaningful for you on your own." We incorporated this rest period for grades K–8 when we started the Greenfield Centre School—it's been a tradition for 17 years. And we recommend it now as part of the Responsive Classroom.

When I asked Wood why this rest time was important for nourishing the soul of students, he replied that "it honors the circadian rhythm of children and grownups and allows them to be present for the rest of the day." He reflected for a moment, then concluded: "We honor the soul when we pay attention to the most sacred parts of our rhythms and bodies."

Silence and Emotional Intelligence

❧ *For no reason, sometimes I can go from being extremely content and happy to feeling frustrated and insecure. All it takes is one little thing to set me off, and then, for the next hour or so, I'll be moping around. I don't understand who I am sometimes—and it's scary.*

❧ *When will I know what myself or being myself really is?*

❧ *Why am I so angry for no reason?*

❧ *Why can I be cruel to others? Why do I let stress build up?*

❧ *Why do I have so much trouble falling asleep?*

❧ *Why are my moods changing constantly?*

Beyond the "rest" for the nervous system, how does silence nourish students' spiritual development? Silence and stillness are a chance to restore equilibrium. *"How do I find balance between the demands of the world? My inner needs for rest, rejuvenation, and simply being?"* writes one student. *"How do others find peace?"* wonders another. A structured period of silence can bring the calm, serenity, and detached perspective that these students are seeking to reorder their lives. "Silence produces peace," says a Swahili proverb, "and peace produces safety."

But silence does not always bring peace. Silence may also be a chance to encounter the turmoil within and begin to sort it out. The ability to identify our own feelings is a basic capacity in emotional intelligence—the foundation of all other emotional and social skills.

Brief periods of silent reflection allow us to sift and sort our feelings, thoughts, and sensations. As we "witness" the state of our emotions, we can discover the equilibrium that is a precondition for social and emotional capacities essential to all learning:

- Understanding and managing one's own emotions.
- Recognizing the emotions of others as distinct from one's own.
- Managing and reducing stress.
- Becoming ready to focus on new information.

Many students, especially in adolescence, have not learned how to manage their feelings: *"Why do I become so immensely filled with thought and feeling that it seems uncontrollable?"* a student writes. *"Why don't I ever take time to think?"* Structured opportunities of silence give them this chance to check in, to discover feelings and thoughts that might otherwise be buried under the commotion of activity and constant interaction with others and with technology.

Because an inability to focus has become a common symptom of today's students, impairing their ability to learn in any discipline, methods that enhance concentration are essential. Silence, solitude, stillness, and muscle relaxation or breathing exercises are practices that can promote these capacities. Such strategies can be as simple as offering one minute of silence or perhaps serene music as each class begins. In *The Mozart Effect,* Don Campbell cites research that suggests that certain music can even help children with attention-deficit disorder (ADD) and attention-deficit disorder with hyperactivity (ADHD) to shift brain wave patterns and display "better focus and mood control, diminished impulsivity, and improved social skills" (Campbell, 1997, p. 233).

For students from some families, theological beliefs give rise to concern about a still and silent mind; for example, "An idle mind is the devil's playground." To respect and support students with such beliefs, a more structured approach to silence is useful in the classroom: "You may use this time to clear your mind, or to notice what you're feeling and thinking right now, or to digest what happened in your last class. You might use this quiet time to pray, or to set a goal for our time together, or to rest."

Chris Gerzon (interview, 1999) created the "Golden Moment"—a daily ritual in her kindergarten early in each day—to help her students develop an appreciation of silence and to encourage their concentration for learning:

Before Golden Moment, we tense and relax our muscles, starting at our feet and going up to our heads. Then we tense every muscle in our bodies and relax every muscle.

"Close your eyes if you can for this Golden Moment," I invite them, "and then breathe in good feelings through your nose and blow out bad feelings through your mouth. Breath in happy feelings and blow out sad. Breath in peaceful and blow out mad." I count one, two, three and then it's over.

For some students, it takes all year just to become comfortable with closing their eyes. Some take a couple of months to learn to sit still. In the beginning, some of them pantomime falling asleep—they lie down and pretend to snore. I tell them, "It's not about sleep—we're taking a recess in our minds. And you can think about whatever you want."

Gerzon reports that her students love the ritualistic repetition: "If I forget to say, 'Stretch your neck,' one of them will call it out." Offering this practice in silence for over 20 years, she has seen the benefits herself but also watches her tiny pupils become aware of the value of silence. One little girl told her that she had been unable to get to sleep at night because she was so afraid. Then she decided to take her own Golden Moment, and she fell asleep. "I had never told my students that this is something you can use when you're scared," said Gerzon. "She had discovered it on her own."

As teachers, we can structure such opportunities for silence to enhance learning and cultivate resilience. We can also honor the often-maligned "lapse" into daydreaming—which can be a rare visit for today's children to the land of imagination. "Whenever I see a kid doing nothing in school," says John Gato (personal communication, 1998), "I'm careful never to shock the reverie out of existence."

Occasionally giving our students time and permission to daydream in their silence can satisfy this need for rest and respite from constant pressure and for flexing and strengthening an imagination weakened by modern life. "So often when a child looks out the window, we say she's off task," says Nel Noddings (cited in Halford, 1998). "Well, she may be on the biggest task of her life" (p. 31). In a world filled with ready-made, fast-paced, and highly stimulating electronic images, silence, for many students, provides a fertile ground for imagination to have its play.

Introducing Silence into the Classroom

❧ *With so much communication, why isn't silence honored more often?*

❧ *Why am I so quiet—why can't I think of things to say, while others can't stop?*

Teachers at all grade levels have found that inviting silence early in a class or school day helps students to settle and focus their minds for learning. In middle and high school where students move from one subject area to another, a few minutes of silence at the beginning of a class can also allow students to digest what they just learned so they can prepare to focus on something new.

Silence can also enhance learning during the middle of a class. A teacher might call for a minute of silence when introducing a new theme for student response, such as at the beginning of a sharing circle, or before a dialogue or debate. After setting the theme, the teacher gives students time for reflection on what they may want to say and for preparing to be focused listeners. Parker Palmer creates moments of silence in the middle of class by resisting the usual urge to rush to response when a question is asked. Attuned to the soul of learning, this gifted professor does not need to rescue students or himself from the "awkwardness" we have come to associate with silence in our classrooms. Instead, he lets the question float in silence, stirring more thought and feeling in the room.

Also, in the middle of class "when the words start to tumble out upon each other and the problem we are trying to unravel is getting more tangled,"writes Palmer (1993), "I try to help my students learn to spot those moments and settle into a time of quiet reflection in which the knots might come untied. We need to abandon the notion that 'nothing is happening' when it is silent, to see how much new clarity a silence often brings" (p. 80).

More and more researchers are discovering the important learning that goes on when "nothing is happening" in the classroom. "Down time," once considered *wasting time,* is now seen as a rich opportunity for consolidating learning and memory. Referring to down time as "wait time," researchers have long recognized these brief periods of silence deliberately introduced by teachers as significantly enhancing cognitive functioning (Stahl, 1994). Recent brain research also suggests, according to Eric Jensen (1998) in *Teaching with the Brain in Mind,* that "learning can become more functional when external stimuli is [sic] shut down" (p. 47). Periods of silent reflection not only soothe the soul but allow the associations, consolidation, and "imprinting" needed for effective learning.

Teachers can also offer silence at the end of each class or the day, to allow students to digest what they have learned and lived that day. Silence allows the brain to more quickly and efficiently process the vast amounts of information, stimulation, and change children face every hour and every day at school and at home. And in a class where students have experienced a significant meeting of hearts and minds, a silent closing can reverberate with a sense of community.

When students are frenetically wound up, simple silence may not be enough to quiet a racing mind. Then a few breathing exercises may work. A highly structured breathing exercise helps many students focus. "Breath in to the count of 1," it begins. "Now out to the count of 2. Breath in to the count of 2 (pause), now out to the count of 4." And so on, until the students are breathing in to the count of 6 and out to the count of 12. And then we go back down in sequence to count 1/count 2. This exercise floods the brain with oxygen and quiets the mind. In communities where families are averse to any breathing exercise that might resemble meditation as a violation of their religious practices, such a highly structured and mathematical "oxygen break" can respect those concerns while providing students with a physiological tool for refreshing their minds.

Enhancing the capacity to learn, to cope, and to relate, silence and stillness also nourish the soul. "The vessel in which soul-making takes place is an inner container scooped out by reflection and wonder," writes Moore (1992, p. 286). One of my seniors used an image remarkably similar to Moore's vessel to evoke the importance of stillness. She explained why she had brought in an empty bottle to represent what was most important to her:

> I like the emptiness of the bottle. It does have a top and I've thought of filling it with something from time to time, but I decided I like its emptiness because it reminds me I don't always have to fill everything, don't always have to fill my time with one activity after another.
>
> I don't always have to be doing and accomplishing all the time, the way I used to think I had to live. I can just be. Just be empty. There's beauty in that, too.

The gifts of silence are intertwined; they cannot really be separated into cognitive, psychological, physiological, or spiritual.

Silence provides young people a chance to make the deep connection to themselves that goes beyond emotional skills to reach the core of their identity. *"Who am I?"* is a recurrent question in the "mysteries" students write. *"What, of all I feel and believe, is truly my own? Is there anything left beyond that which others have implanted within me?"* These questions cry for some way, some time to discover, build, and refine a truly personal inner life.

Stepping out of the fray for a moment, students can begin to gain some distance, some perspective on what they feel so they will be less reactive in social situations. They can begin to realign themselves to their deeper values and personal strengths and return to the community of the classroom renewed.

Periods of silent reflection are essential to goal-setting and decision-making exercises or for self-inventory activities designed to identify and strengthen components of personal identity. The freedom from peer stimulation or pressure allows students easier access to their own values, beliefs, priorities, goals, and sense of purpose. In academic classes that encourage students to link subject themes to their own lives, quiet reflection will enrich "journaling" exercises, essays, or discussions that allow students to express these connections.

Colleen Conrad (interview, 1999) explored a radical use of silence to build community in a classroom that felt completely out of control:

> It was my most difficult class—the low-skilled, high-risk students who have no desire to be in school. When I missed three weeks because of my surgery, this group lost all feeling of community. They created a disruptive, antisocial community that kept any learning from taking place.
>
> When I came back, I told them how that behavior had been so disappointing to me and that there was no way any learning could take place as long as the negative behavior controlled the class. I told them I needed us to pull together once again as a positive community, but no one was ready to do that—they had slid into thinking that failure was inevitable.
>
> So I took a radical step. We spent one full week in silence. I put assignments on the board for students to work on individually. But the real thrust of the week was that we would use silence as an opportunity to decide what our common direction would become.
>
> It was hard for me to participate in such extended silence because I believe so strongly in interactive learning. However, I also believed we would never form as a community unless we took the time to reflect on our vision and goals and determine what had been counterproductive in the behaviors while I was gone.

After a week of silence (and the kids really were silent), we had a sharing circle about what they had decided during the week of reflection. Several of them said they liked the silence—that it was easier to concentrate and that they appreciated having "space" for themselves. What they didn't like was the lack of interaction between them and me. So we talked about how we could have both.

These students basically reestablished class norms—they discovered what the atmosphere needed to be for people to be able to learn, how personal space was to be respected, and the appropriate ways to express concerns or ask for help. They also verbalized specifically what kinds of help they needed from me in order to learn.

Encountering Resistance

All students may have an initial awkwardness with silence that is easily overcome with clear guidance from the teacher. We can affectionately tolerate or even encourage the giggles that may fill the first moments of silence before students can settle in. I have found that exaggerating the giggles or squirming is more effective for achieving stillness than trying to suppress them.

When Conrad first broached the idea of what she called "solo" time, her 8th graders were skeptical.

"Why should we be totally silent?" they wondered. "I can't sit and think about nothing."

So I started with very small chunks: a minute, then two—tiny chunks of doing absolutely nothing. They could keep their eyes open or close them. I told them they could do anything they wanted in the silent stillness: prayer, meditation, even sleep. But I didn't want them problem solving or doing anything active. And I had one important boundary: They had to clear their desks so they wouldn't have immediate access to things that might distract them.

At this stage, Conrad was introducing a "receptive" reflection, in which students learns to clear their minds. Later, she turned to a more "active" mode of reflection:

I started giving them a topic that related to something we were doing in class—a theme or question to reflect on. So when we were reading stories from different cultures that focused on family relations, I asked them during their solo to think about their favorite family member. What are some memories that really in-

voke happy or pleasant feelings? Think about specific times that
brought you the warmest feelings.

Conrad followed the solo with journaling and then reading the
story. She found that the students loved being able to clarify their own
thoughts and experiences *before* being influenced by the text. Then she
would have them go back to their journals and refine what they wrote
in light of what they learned and felt from the story.

> Now when I tell them we're going to take a five-minute solo,
> they are at ease. One girl recently asked me, "Why can't we take a
> solo for a whole period sometime?"

In my own work with students who are afraid of silence or stillness,
becoming anxious and agitated by such nonactivity, artwork is one alternative. Engaging the hands while quieting the mind, drawing, or
sculpting with clay do not disrupt the opportunity for the rest of the
class to experience stillness.

Guided muscle relaxation exercises are another way for some hy-
peractive students to experience moments of profound relief from
their constant motion. The first time I introduced a relaxation exercise
to my 7th grade students one year, I was concerned about Daniel.

An exceptionally bright child, Daniel cannot sit still. My col-
leagues in the middle school are at wit's end with his constant motion:
climbing pipes, hopping on desks and counters, roaming about the room.

Unlike some of my colleagues, I have little tolerance for chaos in the
classroom. But this year, I learn to tolerate Daniel's movement except when
it puts someone in danger. Now as I introduce an exercise that requires absolute stillness and silence, I have little hope that it will work for Daniel. And
I fear he will disrupt the opportunity of every other student to experience
this stress-management tool.

I take him aside. "Daniel, this next exercise might not work for you. I'd
like you to try it, but if you feel restless, I want you to let me know so I can
give you some markers and paper and you can sit just outside the door
drawing until I let you know we're finished." I know that despite his physical agitation, Daniel is a boy I can trust to wait safely out in the hall for a few
minutes.

He is curious. Given the freedom to opt out if he needed to, Daniel
stretches out on the carpeted floor along with the other students. I take the
students calmly through a progression of tensing and releasing each major
muscle group and encourage them to use deep breathing. When we finish,
I give them two or three minutes of silence to enjoy the feeling of being re-

laxed. To my surprise, Daniel never stirs. And when we get to the silence, I see him lying comfortably in absolute stillness.

When we complete the exercise, Daniel comes running up to me with a beautiful smile on his intense little face. "That was so cool!" he says, his dark eyes flashing. " I was still—did you see? I was really still. It felt so good. I can't remember ever feeling that still."

Silence Is for Teachers, Too

Can we really introduce our students to the joy of silence if we ourselves as teachers have avoided this experience in the way we run our busy lives? I build encounters with silence and solitude into every training session I offer teachers, even when it means "not covering the material" as fully as I would like. I do so because, in every session, one or two teachers say something like "I learned something from that silence that's going to change the rest of my life."

When he worked as a principal, Chip Wood (interview, 1999) discovered how essential it was to provide his faculty with opportunities for silence.

> It was the year that Massachusetts passed a law that there would be a moment of silence at the beginning of each school day—it was their way of handling the prayer-in-school controversy. We found we liked it so much that we also put in a moment of silence at lunch before we ate. I talked with teachers about how to talk with their students about these moments—about the difference between thinking and reflection.
>
> Then I realized that if the state of Massachusetts is going to require the students to have a moment of silence, then I'm going to require our faculty to have a moment. So I told my teachers that 10 minutes before the buses come, we're going to come together for a moment of silence and then share in a circle for 5 minutes. I was told that five principals later at that school, that faculty still gathers in silence and sharing each morning.

Like Wood, I discovered that as teachers, we need ample practice with silence ourselves if we are to introduce it effectively into the classroom.

Periods of silence can help teachers more broadly prepare for welcoming soul into the classroom. Sometimes we come into class preoccupied with emotional issues or exhausted by a conflict. If we can clear our minds and hearts and refresh our spirits, we can be more responsive to our students. Most of our issues—a fight with a colleague, a personal family matter, a troubling dream—are too private to share appropriately with our students. We do not want to use our students as our own support system. Particularly at a time when so many children are being enrolled to parent their own parents, students need adult role models who can care gracefully for their own needs without imposing them on children. Silence is not the only place to take our own stress—sometimes it is essential to talk with a colleague, friend, or counselor. But silence can offer much solace and "sorting" time for teachers.

In addition to sitting quietly in the morning at home, I try to take a few minutes before each class to take stock of what I am feeling and clear my mind. In those minutes before class—in an office, my car, even a closet in an empty classroom—I imagine the class I am about to work with. I see myself looking into each pair of eyes, imagining my heart opening to each child. Then I can often remember issues important to the group or to particular students—emotional issues separate from my carefully prepared lesson plan. I also focus on deep breathing to clear my mind and oxygenate my brain, or do several minutes of "forced" yawning which refreshes my brain and allows me to be alert and receptive to my students. When I work with a partner, we sometimes take a moment of silence to become present and aligned with each other.

Some educators add structure to the simplicity of silence. Though I am not recommending teaching meditation to students (see Chapter 7), teachers can use this tool to build their own tolerance for silence and stillness. Jack Miller, a professor at the Ontario Institute for Studies in Education at the University of Toronto, has introduced more than 850 teachers to meditation practice. Experienced teachers between 30 and 55 years old, most of these teachers have never meditated before. "Only two students have asked not to do the meditation," reports Miller, who introduces four or five basic approaches to meditation. "My courses are electives and the enrollment is always filled with a waiting list of others wanting to get in. I believe that many students now take the course *because* of the meditation requirement" (Miller, J., 1999, p. 124).

Many teachers have shared with me their own approaches to cultivating the clear mind and open heart that silence often brings: running, hiking, playing a musical instrument or listening to music, painting, meditating, writing poetry, or keeping a daily journal. All these processes allow us to refresh our minds and make room for feeling and spirit to come into our teaching.

Solitude

- ❧ *How can I change feeling lonely?*
- ❧ *Will I feel safe next year being alone and not having anyone know where I am all the time?*
- ❧ *I wonder how I'm going to survive as a strong individual when from every direction are people and forces that are trying to influence and change me into something less me and more them.*
- ❧ *How does one learn to trust oneself, to believe in oneself?*
- ❧ *Can I escape my own evil/darkness?*
- ❧ *How can I learn to not share everything about myself, I mean, how can I learn to hold some of me sacred?*

We can enhance all the benefits of silence—insight, renewal, and discovery—by brief periods of solitude. Classroom teachers may simulate solitude by certain forms of silence. For students who are able to focus and concentrate, periods of silent reflection, combined with stillness, writing, or artistic expression, take them into a world unto themselves. For students who were never given the opportunity as small children to develop the capacity for solitude, periods of silence in a safe and loving classroom may introduce them to solitude. Children originally learn the capacity to be alone in the presence of another—usually the mother. Only when children feel the security of a solid attachment to a caretaker can they risk even beginning to develop an autonomous self. Donald Winnicott (cited in Storr, 1988) writes: "I am trying to justify the paradox that the capacity to be alone is based on the experience of being alone in the presence of someone, and that without a sufficiency of this experience the capacity to be alone cannot develop" (p. 20).

Common Misperceptions

Like silence, solitude evokes fear in some young people, but is a rare solace for most. Before offering solitude as a potential balm or catalyst for soul, we can explore with young people first the negative meanings of being alone in our culture.

Students often perceive of solitude as punishment; indeed, people in authority use it that way for both children and adults. In U.S. prisons, "solitary confinement" is the worst punishment short of death. In earlier times, sending someone off alone was often an act of banishment from the warmth of the community, exile from home, outcast from friend and family. "Time out" at home and at school is often commanded in anger. And young people estranged from themselves or others often associate solitude with restlessness, boredom, and loneliness.

So first we must ensure that we are not using silence or solitude to induce shame or isolation. When Conrad told me the story about creating an entire week of what she called "solo time" for her most disruptive class, I knew that only because this teacher's love for her students is so palpable, her kindness so constant, could they see the solitude as an opportunity for discovery, not punishment.

Next, we should distinguish loneliness from solitude, because young people often confuse the two. We might lead a dialogue about Thoreau's statement: "We are for the most part more lonely when we go abroad among men than when we stay in our chambers."

When we have raised awareness about the negative associations that go with solitude, we can begin to offer experiences aimed at developing the capacity to be alone, to nourish the self.

How to Use Solitude

In addition to showing students that solitude can be a balm for stress, we can introduce it as a way to grow their own identity. "The capacity to be alone thus becomes linked with self-discovery and self-realization; with becoming aware of one's deepest needs, feelings and impulses" (Storr, 1988, p. 21). We need not confuse *self-awareness* with an ethic of selfishness or self-absorption. Rather, we need to create opportunities for students to strengthen a core identity that is the source of creativity, of living a life of meaning and purpose. A strong identity is actually a precondition for generosity to others. Taking time to be alone is an essential step in addressing questions like these: *"How can I be 'myself' more?" "How can I believe what I need to believe without alienating my family?"* and *"How will I define myself without my family?"*

Paradoxically, strengthening this autonomous self is what allows students to form meaningful relationships with others—to understand the interrelationships between being an individual and belonging to a group, between autonomy and intimacy. "We are not capable of union with another on the deepest level," said Thomas Merton (cited in Miller, J., 1999), "until the inner self in each one of us is sufficiently awakened to confront the inmost spirit of the other" (p. 25).

It may be difficult to awaken this inner self in students who have rarely experienced love and affirmation for who they are. *"How do others find the courage to express themselves?"* writes one student, struggling with this question of authenticity. Students who are desperate for approval may construct a "false self" based almost entirely on pleasing others. For young people like this, silence and solitude may force a painful confrontation with a hollowness within. This is one reason it is so essential that we offer these experiences with a great deal of gentleness, encouragement, and patience—and, ultimately, the opportunity to "opt out" for students who appear threatened by these practices.

Respect for Privacy and Personal Timing

Respecting a student's own sense of timing for self-awareness is another way that we can honor and strengthen "solitude." I learned this most powerfully from Alice, a senior who, for 16 weeks, never spoke in class.

With spiked dyed-black hair, bright red lipstick, and black clothes always cut too low on top and too high below, Alice tested the limits daily. One day when she didn't show up for class, I learned that she had been sent home because of her provocative attire.

Alice also pushed the limits of my principle of "respecting privacy." On the five-day wilderness retreat, when even the most reticent students would find their voices, Alice never spoke out. I was sad not to hear from her because I had heard that she was exceptionally bright and creative in her academic classes.

When other students began to complain about her silence in the later weeks of our Senior Passages class, I came to her defense. "I'm glad you've expressed how it makes you feel when Alice doesn't speak. . . . But Alice is always here—she listens attentively and does nothing to disrupt our conversations. I think we need to honor her right to choose when she's ready to speak."

In those years, we ended the course with a closing ceremony called a "Giveaway." All the students brought something that had been meaningful to them that they now felt ready to let go of as an expression of moving on from childhood. They placed the objects on a blanket in the center; and one by one, each student would choose something to take with them and ask the giver to share the story.

When I saw the package of condoms on the blanket, I immediately thought Alice had brought them. I assumed she would say nothing, as usual, or perhaps say something perverse. The condoms were "chosen" last. Nothing else was left.

Indeed, Alice had brought them. When asked what they meant to her, she began to speak: "I brought these because they symbolize a life style I was caught up in most of these last years we've all known each other. A life style of cheap and easy sex, superficial relationships.

"I've found something deeper in my life recently. I've discovered what it feels like to really be loved by someone and to feel a depth of love inside me for another person. I know this is something you would understand," she continued, looking around at the class.

"I am ready to let go of my old ways. I already have. This ritual just gives me a chance to name what I already know."

When the semester was over, Alice was finally ready to speak. Emerging from the cocoon of her own healing process, she trusted us with her truth. Had we violated the rhythm of her own growth by forcing her to participate, she would have resisted and shut us out. Instead of deepening the connection in this group, she might have sabotaged it. Because we honored her privacy—her solitude and silence—she shared her wisdom with us, and her courage to change.

The gateway of silence and solitude challenges our assumptions about the concept of participation. Many teachers grade students as if participation equals talking. During activities that invite heart and soul into the classroom, we must reexamine and redefine "participation" to emphasize *engagement* and *attentiveness* rather than *talking* and *doing*. If we pressure students to address any theme we raise or engage in every activity we suggest, we risk trampling on the fragile boundaries of the child's growing sense of self.

Many teachers find that a journal is a way to protect the solitude of their students, while also tracking the student's quality of presence in class. Students who choose silence with their peers are often willing to allow the teacher to read reflections that they write on the topic at the end of the class. "I have a couple of kids who don't say anything in class," says Elissa Weindling (personal communication, 1999), a teacher at University Heights High School in the Bronx. "In their journals, they write things that are very deep and show that they've been really connecting."

At the beginning of the semester, Weindling and her colleagues provide their students with a format for their journal reflections. They offer a page full of questions like these:

- What did you do well today?
- Is there anything you wish you had done differently?
- What was hard to talk about? Why?
- Was this a good topic for you?
- Did anyone say something that upset you?

The teachers offer these questions as "prompts" to guide students' writing at the end of each class. Some teachers give students a handout with a few specific questions.

"I tell them they don't need to share their journals—they can mark off sections they don't want me to read," says Weindling. "I do have to collect them and check that they're writing." Most of her students trust Weindling with their solitary thoughts. But sometimes, a student feels adamant about her privacy:

> "I don't want you to read anything at all," said Tasha. Each week, I would talk with her about the topics we had discussed and ask, "Do you mind if I read about this question?" She would say, "Sure, that one's okay." For weeks, I would ask about each topic separately, and she would always say, "Okay." After about three weeks, she realized that she felt comfortable letting me read everything.

Like Alice, Tasha needed to *choose* when to be alone and when to connect. Having a teacher who was willing to respect her solitude and offer her that choice over and over again was precisely the key to building both autonomy and trust in others.

Respecting the solitude of our students also means protecting them from the probing questions of their peers. Appropriate questioning is a complex issue for teachers trying to teach social skills because the ability to ask meaningful questions is a valuable skill in problem-solving and forming friendships. Students may question one another out of genuine concern and interest. As teachers, we may do the same, and the power of our position can make our questions feel even more intrusive to the student. We can remind our students often that they can choose to not answer a question that feels like a violation of their privacy. No simple formula exists here—but the climate of a classroom shifts when both teachers and students value the principle of solitude.

The Benefits of Solo Time

Educators have created opportunities for students to experience solitude through "solo" activities built into field trips, outdoor education, adventure-learning trips, or rites of passage.

Although students often have a profound awakening to their inner life in an overnight solo, I have been amazed at the richness of self-discovery that occurs during even a 45-minute "alone time." I give some of these solo "assignments" along with specific questions or exercises designed to help the students make contact with their feelings, goals, values, or decisions. Other solo instructions may ask the students to experience the emptiness of no structure and notice what comes up from inside to fill the vacuum. Such experiences, while not always easy or fun or "spiritually nourishing" for students at first, give teenagers a chance to discover wisdom, creativity, or perhaps greater clarity about a problem they need to resolve. Brian and Anne Marie shared their appreciation for their solo times at a retreat:

"The solo time was really important to me," says Brian, "and that may sound strange from a guy who, trust me, really hates being alone. For a long time, my mind was just blank and that was pretty unusual. Then I started to think about my mother."

Brian's mother died when he was 10 after a long struggle with the crippling effects of an accident. He rarely spoke of her in class, except to explain briefly why he lived with his aunt.

"I had a conversation with her," he continues. He smiles. "I mean, she didn't really talk back, but I got to say certain things to her. And then I played—like a little child—I just played among the rocks and the trees. I can't remember the last time I got to feel like a child."

"I thought I'd hate it," says Ann Marie. "But I didn't. I'm going off to the West Coast for college; and I realized, this may be the last time for a while that I'll see snow, that I'll be so close to the elk, that I'll be with this kind of beauty. And I prayed a lot. I don't often take time for that, and it felt so good."

Although making a genuine connection to our inner selves seems to be enhanced by a dramatic shift of getting away from ordinary life, many students can find opportunities for solitude *at home or at school.* One colleague of mine worked with seniors in a high school in Brooklyn located on a community college campus. She had no resources to design an off-campus retreat into their course. So during one of their class sessions, she asked the students to use the campus itself for a brief solo. This simple encounter with solitary reflection in the outdoors was provocative for some, peaceful for others.

Even the confines of the classroom can stir the creativity of teachers in giving students a taste of solitude. Totally engrossed in activities that encourage reflection and expression through writing or art, a student can connect to his inner self even in the company of others. Through these solitary activities, students discover and express their own feelings, values, and beliefs. Telling students "This is a time for you to be alone, even though we're in a busy classroom" can awaken or affirm students' hunger for a rich inner life.

Many young people never have the opportunity to be alone. Students may be afraid when they are first asked to encounter either solitude or stillness. Linnea, for example, spent her entire solo assignment dwelling on her fear of being alone. Afterward, she recounted the layers of fear she peeled away in the course of less than an hour, alone in a tree as close to our group meeting site as possible. Facing and itemizing her fears, this student was clearing away the debris that was preventing a deep connection to herself. Adolescents who stave off this encounter as long as possible are not only missing an opportunity for spiritual development, but jeopardizing the formation of an identity that is essential to growing up and growing strong.

Cautions and Exceptions

As teachers, we must watch for students who may be exceptions; for example, students who have experienced a violent trauma may be terrified of solitude. They may be wise to avoid it. And though we might try to gently encourage a student who is resisting this assignment, we must be careful not to push students to override their own wisdom and self-protection. Recently, in a workshop I gave for adults who work with young people, one man told us that he was tormented during the one hour of solitude I assigned after lunch, despite the natural beauty of the retreat center. "When I'm alone and not doing something active, I get flashbacks to Vietnam. I can't help it. Even in a pretty place like this. So I'm careful to avoid being alone."

I apologized. The path of growth and healing is not well served by forcing someone to reactivate an old trauma. I realized that some students may be less vocal about or even less directly aware of the nightmares that might await them in solitude. If a student seems to be agitated about time alone or is staying close by when others are scattering to their solo sites, a teacher's gentleness and respect will serve them far more than being forced to adhere to a class assignment.

One response to this challenge is to create, early in the semester, a tradition of the "witness" role—a thoughtful observer who reports back to the group. We explain to the students:

• Witnesses see and hear things those engaged in an activity will never notice.

• Witnesses are not just passive observers but actively support the group with their caring.

Once we establish the role of the witness, we can invite one or two participants to volunteer as observers of any activity that seems in any way problematic. Students may also request this role. This gives a graceful and legitimate reprieve for students who truly need to step out; it also provides the group with the insights that come from an active observer.

We know we have succeeded in tapping into a real yearning of the soul when students begin to see for themselves the power of solitude in bringing individual peace and harmony in the classroom. Colleen Conrad describes such a turning point:

> This 8th grade English class meets just before lunch. The kids are hungry, and the class is so big that no one has much personal space. It's a heterogeneous mix, so I have kids with special needs in the group, as well as students who are quite bright and everything in between. I've struggled with this class because there's so much "negative" energy created simply because of those physical conditions.
>
> We have been doing solos two or three times a week for over a month. One day, the class is simply unable to focus; everyone is restless and fidgety. Nothing works. Then Jessica blurts out, "We need a solo time. Why haven't you given us a solo time?"
>
> I realize that this student has identified exactly what is needed. So I stop and ask the class. They agree. Almost immediately, the kids clear their desks, close their eyes, and I can almost hear the collective sigh of relief.
>
> We solo for about five minutes. When I call the group back together, everyone (literally, *everyone*) is calm. We go back to our work, and the rest of the class period works beautifully.

"This movement from the outer to the inner and back again is a basic human rhythm," writes Bernie Neville (1989) in *Educating Psyche*. Just like adults who jog or meditate, "children also need the opportunity to turn inward, not only to grow as balanced, healthy individuals but also to learn effectively what they are being taught" (p. 18).

Encouraging our students to go "inward and downward," we provide the empty spaces crucial to consolidating learning. Given the "outward and upward" thrust of modern culture and education, it takes courage for teachers to initiate this gateway. When we are willing to persist through resistance and even ridicule, silence and solitude can become catalysts for deep connection and for the search for meaning and purpose, for transcendence, joy, and creativity.

Certainly this gateway can be a means to other ends in nourishing the souls of our students. But even for students who go no further, we have seen the powerful effect on spiritual development, learning, and the building of community when students are give the chance to stop the noise, quiet the mind, and still the body.

4 *Meaning and Purpose*

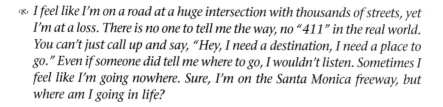

> ❧ *I feel like I'm on a road at a huge intersection with thousands of streets, yet I'm at a loss. There is no one to tell me the way, no "411" in the real world. You can't just call up and say, "Hey, I need a destination, I need a place to go." Even if someone did tell me where to go, I wouldn't listen. Sometimes I feel like I'm going nowhere. Sure, I'm on the Santa Monica freeway, but where am I going in life?*

The powerful "road" metaphor in this senior's mysteries question captures the deep search that many students undertake to find meaning and purpose in their lives. Adolescence is a time when big questions—what the French call *les profondeurs*—begin to surface with volcanic urgency. These existential questions are so deep that we can never find the bottom. Certainly by the time a child enters adolescence, "each senses mystery in the cosmos and needs relationship to that mystery" (Gurian, 1998, p. 264). Without such connection, our experience of life can be meaningless, what William James called a "blooming, buzzing confusion" (cited in Sloan, 1994, p. 12).

I've found that adolescents make a subtle but critical difference between their search for meaning and their yearning for purpose. Questions of *purpose*—what will give meaning to *my own life*—arise in students' questions about their future and their goals and in their struggle to define what is most important to them:

❧ *Are any of my goals worthwhile?*
❧ *What do I really want to do?*
❧ *What's God's will for my life?*
❧ *What is my destiny?*

❧ *What purpose do my enemies serve?*

Students also ponder what gives *meaning to life itself:*

❧ Is there a meaning to life?
❧ *How far will they look into space for the meaning of life till they find it in God?*
❧ *I want to have myself know that we do matter in at least our small span of time on earth.*
❧ *Do things happen for a reason?*
❧ *Is the meaning I give to life from happiness and love merely chemicals programmed to make me feel that way, or the true meaning? Or is meaning, life, etc. what you make it?*

In their questions, students reveal a longing to connect to some larger, ongoing frame of meaning. "Soul is at home in a sense of time that reaches beyond the limits of ordinary human life," writes Thomas Moore (1992). "The soul is interested in eternal issues, even as it is embedded in the particulars of ordinary life. This, the interpenetration of time and eternity, is one of the great mysteries explored by many religions . . . and mythologies" (p. 223).

Through their stories, students reveal their need for an enduring frame of meaning. Through religious beliefs or connection to lineage or nature; through concepts of social justice, evolution, or progress; or through creative expression, students respond to "the challenge of finding or composing some kind of order, unity and coherence in the force fields of our lives" (Fowler, 1991, p. 24). When we as teachers create opportunities at school for students to articulate these frames of meaning, we can substantially contribute to their spiritual development.

"It's not important where you think the soul is; it's what you're looking for with it, that's important," said a 13-year-old girl to Robert Coles (1990). In *The Spiritual Life of Children,* Coles discovered in children an "intense, penetrating rumination" (pp. 301–302) that moved him deeply.

But without a compassionate, inquisitive adult like Coles in their lives, where do most children get this opportunity to express these urgent mysteries or the "clues" they are finding along the way?

Before we explore the opportunities in the classroom for meaning and purpose, we must ask why educators rarely welcome students' "big questions" into the classroom. What happens if there is no forum, no safe place for young people to air their questions? What are the consequences for students when schools exclude their quest for meaning from the curriculum?

Loss of Meaning: How It Affects Learning and Risk

✎ *Why do people commit suicide when they're not in trouble?*

✎ *Am I really doing the things that are going to make me happy, or are they for my mother or for the values of our society?*

✎ *What is the use of going to school, earning money and so on, if all that happens after all your effort is death?*

✎ *Why do people feel business brings fulfillment and partying brings happiness?*

✎ *Am I here for a reason, or do I just create reasons in order to not go crazy?*

✎ *How can I NOT be a cynic?*

Without meaning in their lives, students' motivation to learn is imperiled. Many students today cannot focus, listen, or even feel the will to learn. Helping these students find their own motivation is increasingly important. Young people who have the opportunity to discover what has meaning for *them* and who feel they are going somewhere in life can be more easily engaged in learning and persisting through obstacles and setbacks. "Deep meanings are the source of most intrinsic motivation," write Renate and Geoffrey Caine (1997) in *Education on the Edge of Possibility.* "They are the source of our reasons to keep going even when we do not understand" (p. 112).

Not only motivation but the learning process itself relies on the student's ability to make meaningful connections, to discover and create patterns of meaning. Though many educators understand the importance of meaning at this level, they still find it difficult to make a place in school for "meaning" in its more mysterious, ultimate levels. As the Caines (1997) write:

> To advocate teaching for meaning and then to deny students the opportunity to explore and ask the most profound questions about how what they are learning relates to a meaningful life is absurd. . . .
>
> In our opinion, the gateways will be really opened for individuals to "become what they can be" when the deep and profound questions are invited into education. . . . Clearly, we are now at the meeting ground of science; spirituality; and in many countries, the law and the constitution. These are questions with

which educators and society have to deal, and which require extensive examination in intellectually rich and safe forums (p. 96).

Or, as a recent high school graduate put it, "If you can't ask the big questions, it's like you're building something without a foundation."

Certainly students' will and capacity to learn are impaired when they lack meaning and purpose. This void also puts them at risk in a more fundamental way. It undermines their motivation to *live.* "Millions of children are not safe physically, educationally, economically, or spiritually," writes Marian Wright Edelman (cited in Brendtro et al., 1990). "The poor black youths who shoot up drugs on street corners and the rich white youths who do the same thing in their mansions share a common disconnectedness from any hope or purpose" (p. 26).

Troubled teenagers are often hiding from a sense of emptiness inside, a sense of meaninglessness that comes when social and religious traditions no longer provide a sense of meaning, continuity, and participation in a larger whole. *"Why this emptiness, in this world, in my heart? How does this emptiness get there, go away, and come back again?"* asks one 10th grade student. The vacuum of spiritual guidance and fulfilment in their lives leads to despair and alienation. Only recently are educators and social scientists beginning to see that this absence of meaning is a critical variable in violent and self-destructive behavior in our youth.

Many students have lost even the capacity to ask. They are deflected from their own search by the distortion of meaning when commercial media rush in to fill the void. "Find beauty and meaning in what is external—in what can be bought and sold," croon the advertisers. "Seek satisfaction and connection through drugs and sexuality," urge the images that flood television, film, video games, and the Internet. Such pervasive messages offer our students a seductive and ultimately empty alternative to the existential search.

Social scientists search for the keys to the resilience of young people. Many students thrive; they have the capacity to respond constructively to the challenges, suffering, and unexpected changes inevitable in all lives and tragically prominent in the lives of some children. It is precisely this mysterious capacity that Viktor Frankl (1984) explored in *Man's Search for Meaning.* Frankl asked why some people could physically and spiritually survive horrific experiences that killed or brutalized others. Observing his fellow prisoners in a series of concentration camps, he saw prisoners who endured despite greater physical frailty than those who perished. Delving deeply into their resilience (and his own), he saw people who had a sense of purpose for their lives, people who knew how to put their experiences, even the most inhumane suffering, into a larger context of meaning.

Although the search for meaning is critical to learning and even survival, it has been largely omitted from the schools where our children spend most of their lives. At the college level, philosophy and religion courses offer some students this chance. But for the children and adolescents who crowd our public schools, these questions are often excluded from the curriculum. Many teachers are troubled by such unfathomable dilemmas for which they have no answers. Others believe they *do* have answers; they also know that to provide such answers in schools would violate the First Amendment. So the curriculum rarely makes a place to even pose the questions, leaving young people to fend for themselves. A natural place to explore purpose is in career planning or goal setting. "A senior in high school must make colossal decisions whether he or she is ready or not," writes one student. "The more people can be honest about and aware of their own needs when making these decisions, the healthier the decisions will be."

When career-planning or goal-setting programs foster authentic self-discovery, students become "purposeful"—determined to accomplish their goals. And not only high schoolers—some researchers have seen positive results from such programs for middle school students at high risk for criminal behavior: "If they can be helped to discover their gifts and how these gifts can and will be utilized through work in the future, they begin to feel a sense of purpose that can protect them from criminal behavior even at this young age" (Greenberg, interview, 1996).

But even in lessons on decision making, teachers often ignore the larger questions of personal meaning and purpose in life. Educators teach mechanical techniques that engage the rational mind. They rarely give students tools to access what wisdom they might possess about their life mission.

If we don't cultivate the inner life of adolescents as part of their search for goals or careers, they will likely make their decisions based on external pressures. "So many of my friends are so clueless," writes one senior. "They don't know what they want to do, they know what they're supposed to do. They don't know how they feel, they know how they're supposed to feel." Denied the guidance to penetrate beyond the surface, students can access only what is superficial and obvious.

Peers, parents, teachers—their external expectations and values are paramount in the decision-making process for students who have not had the guidance from teachers to look within for a possible larger sense of purpose. Such goals or career decisions are often unsatisfying and short lived. Schools, academic majors, and careers chosen without passion, without a sense of purpose often lead to high turnover or sticking it out with low motivation; low performance; and, sometimes, physical or psychological disabilities.

How then do we create opportunities for students to search for meaning and purpose? How can we awaken this search in students who may have lost even the ability to ask these questions?

Safely Inviting the Big Questions

❧ *Is there life after death?*

❧ *Does everything have a place in a huge sort of organization where they each play a part or is life random and meaningless? And where is my place?*

❧ *Why are jobs, titles, mainstream success so important?*

❧ *I think to myself all the time, How did life begin on earth? How was life in the beginning, before there were boats, cars, planes? How did these people look, act, feel toward life?*

❧ *I wonder if there is really God up there or someone up there. Because God is supposed to be good and guide you but I have been hurt so many times that I wonder if there really is God.*

❧ *If people/animals die and there isn't heaven, or another place, then what is the point of life and dying and living and the world?*

Simply seeing the universality of these big questions from their peers helps students validate their own questions and nourishes their souls. As we saw in Chapter 1, students embark on a search for meaning and purpose when educators give them the opportunity to *anonymously* write down their questions about themselves and about life. When we read these questions back to the group, we validate our students' quest.

Throughout the curriculum—in literature, history, foreign languages, and science, as well as in social and emotional learning courses—teachers can create a safe environment where students can reveal and explore their bigger questions. In a class for high school seniors called "Society and Nature," science teacher Doug Eaton (interview, 1999) addresses his students' "cosmic" questions in a council meeting held during a field trip they take to an old-growth forest. Fifth-grade teacher Meg Kenny in Vermont begins each school year by encouraging students to write their questions about themselves and the world. "There are always questions about the beginnings of things, conflict and justice, . . . mysteries, and unknowable things" (Mann, 1998, p. 1).

But *creating a safe environment* is the key. Too many teachers ignore or even laugh at the audacity or naiveté of students who ask such questions in the school environment. Sadly, I have watched this kind of behavior dampen and sometimes damage the spirit in students:

Two middle school teachers invite me to observe them "adapt" my approach to their human development curriculum.

Instead of offering their students an opportunity to pose questions anonymously in writing, Bill and Carol corral a large group of students and require them to each ask a question out loud.

"Tell us what you're wondering about these days," instructs Carol. When a student hesitates, she insists: "You must have a question!" Carol asks the group to wait until this reluctant student "participates."

Halfway through this ordeal, one shy and serious girl says brightly, "I wonder about what happens when you die."

"Oh, yeah," Bill guffaws. "We could really get far with that one."

Despite being a compassionate and caring teacher, Bill was so unnerved that he responded to her heartfelt and timeless question by dismissing it with a nervous laugh. In a profession where much of our authority has been predicated on our ability to "know," or to have the "right answer," teachers are often loathe to allow the bigger questions in the classroom.

Questions about personal purpose or the meaning of life can lead to the issue of ultimate causes and religious beliefs. Like Bill, teachers often mishandle such questions or shy away from creating a forum for them. Afraid to violate the First Amendment by imposing our own views, we prefer to avoid these questions altogether. Especially to young children, this can feel like we are discouraging or condemning the quest. Montessori specialist Aline Wolf (1996, pp. 157–162) offers a series of strategies for honoring children's questions about God.

> Instead of setting aside such questions with responses like "I think you should ask your parents," or "We'll talk about that some other time," questions like these should be honored as audible signs of children's developing spirituality. "That's a very good question, Nicky" or "I have often wondered about that myself," is a good response with which to start.

She encourages teachers to express their own uncertainty or sense of mystery without feeling that not knowing in any way undermines their authority. We can also show respect for the views of both believers and nonbelievers without giving priority to any one point of view. As Wolf says:

> When a child asks if God made the world, a response might be, "Some people think that God made the world and other people do not think that God made the world. It's a question that people have been trying to answer for thousands of years. I am glad you are thinking about it, too."

Because most parents care deeply about the primary importance of their own beliefs in shaping their children's development, we can also encourage children to share these questions at home.

Ultimately, Wolf (1996, pp. 157–162) believes that the most useful response to encourage the student's spiritual growth is to "return the question." After letting the child know that we value their search, we can give it back to the child and the other students to draw forth their own wisdom and wonder:

> "That is a question that each of us can think about. Where do you think God is?"
>
> "I think God is up in the sky," a child might reply. And this answer may spark a variety of ideas from other children:
>
> "Maybe God is the sun watching us."
>
> "My Dad says, 'God is in the church.'"
>
> "Maybe God is right here but we can't see Him."

"Returning the question" is the guiding principle I have used in my own work with adolescents to explore these profound mysteries. I have also used activities to encourage students to find their own answers or "clues" to what gives meaning and purpose in their lives. The next sections present some of these activities and highlight opportunities for students to develop a deeper sense of meaning and purpose.

Exploring Individual Purpose

❧ *Why am I here?*

❧ *Does my life have a purpose? How do I find out what it is?*

❧ *I think about my future constantly, hoping I'll be doing something successful.*

∞ *I wonder why people base their life around religion, believing that they cannot form their own destiny, and believing someone will provide for them.*

∞ *Is it better to be very good at several things or to be great at one thing? Is it strange to want to be great at something? Why do I want this?*

∞ *I have a wonderment about my sense of destiny. I would like to know what is in store for the remainder of my life. One fifth of my life has gone by; and unless I make a drastic impact on the world, then I feel my life is in vain.*

∞ *Is there something out there that I can really become passionate about? Something that I love to do?*

∞ *Sometimes I wonder why I am here: What is my significance. Will I someday find the cure for cancer or AIDS? Or was I put here just so I could rescue my neighbor's cat from a tree 20 years from now?*

Although questions of meaning and purpose often intertwine, many students are responsive to activities that focus on their own personal destiny or purpose. To explore their life's mission and to set goals that reflect it is a noble educational goal. But how can it be done? Here are a few approaches that work.

Instead of beginning with lofty words like *mission,* I create a council for my 10th grade students on the subject of success. "How do you define success?" I ask them. "What does it mean to you personally? Tell us a story about your future that helps us understand what might be going on for you when you're feeling like a success?"

When working with seniors, I ask them more directly what they do or don't know about their purpose.

"So many of your mysteries questions are about what you're here for, about your destiny, your future," I say at the beginning of council. "If you *do* know something, what have been the clues? If you *don't* feel you know anything yet, how does that feel?"

"I see a lot of my purpose in people—in the connections I make and the impact I make on people's lives," says Josh.

"I find a lot of my purpose in being a child of God, in my faith, in walking that Way," says Petra, holding the talking stone in one hand and placing the other hand over the cross on her heart. "While God creates and names every single star, he knows my name, thoughts, and needs."

As we go around the circle, most students say something about love. Peter is firm about what is most important in his mission: "My destiny is not to be an astronaut or great politician but to bring love."

Khalil is lost in concepts: "I believe that destiny is not what's going to happen to you in the future but what's happened 'til now to bring you here."

Like Khalil, the idea of destiny is taking Nancy into the past. She is making sense—making meaning—about all the things that brought her to where she is today. "My suffering has been part of my destiny."

From her previous stories, we all know that Nancy had been raped.[1] She had told us that she jammed the memory into her unconscious, never telling anyone, including herself, what happened. A year later she began to suffer from insomnia, then depression. When her thoughts turned to suicide, she went to her parents for help. Within a few weeks of therapy, the memory of the rape came back; and a long healing process began.

"I know it's hard for you guys to believe, but [my suffering] has given me so many gifts already. I think my destiny is to use those gifts somehow—to help others."

"You know that little man I drew when we did that symbol exercise weeks ago?" asks Kenny, looking around the room for nods of recognition. "That little man is my music. And sometimes I hate this little man, and sometimes I love him. I put my bass aside for a time, a long time, thinking, 'I don't like doing music. I'm just gonna stop.' But then it's like I *have* to go back to it. And then when I go back to it, it's like I'm a different person."

"When I think of purpose, I think of power," says Karim. "Not the kind of power that puts other people down. I want the kind of power that lets you do what you want to do with your life."

Cathy, one of the last to speak, has the courage to admit she hasn't given this subject much thought: "I really don't have a clue. But this is interesting, what everyone else is saying. I'm kind of amazed that everyone else has been thinking about this. I've learned a lot, just listening to you guys. I have a feeling it might get me thinking about it myself."

When asked too directly, many young people, like Cathy, cannot easily express what really matters to them. They may even be afraid to know, lest they be disappointed by circumstances that make them feel it's impossible to achieve what they really want. Or they may simply lack tools to access their deeper yearnings. At the simplest level, giving students time for quiet reflection can begin to open these channels. More actively, calling them to envision their futures can sometimes

---

[1]See Chapter 7 and the Conclusion for a discussion of how educators can appropriately and compassionately respond to difficult emotional content—such as rape—that students may raise in class.

help them tap into their deeper values. Teachers at University Heights help students set authentic goals by using an imaginative journey into their futures, including writing their own obituaries. (These teachers had taken an in-depth workshop I provided on working with grief. They are prepared to respond compassionately to issues that might arise in working with this metaphor.)

"I was surprised to see that we had to write our own obituary," wrote Caesar. "At first it was uncomfortable but then it was fun." This senior went on to write:

> Caesar Rivera died today at the age of 100. He was known for his great blockbuster movies. He was a director, producer and writer of most of his own films. . . . He was known for the billions he donated to charity over the years. He began his film study in Brooklyn College. . . . He was married with two kids which will take over as the presidents of his production company.

The obituary of another student in the Bronx took a different turn:

> Martinez, Roberto. Invented the Pentiem III system. . . . He was well known in his community for helping to improve the safety and value of his community. He will be most remembered for his shyish ways and warm heart. Roberto Martinez was known for being there when needed. He had two children and wife which he loved deeply. Roberto will indeed be missed by both his family and the community.

When we help students squarely face the inevitable limits of life, we can motivate students like Roberto and Caesar to think more actively about what really matters to them.

A cumulative process of self-definition occurs in classes where students regularly write or tell stories that relate content themes to stories from their own lives. When students feel that people genuinely listen to them as they share their lives, they begin to sense their own significance as human beings. "Every time that I speak, I feel that I am being listened to and that I am affecting your lives," writes Lisa, a senior in Colorado. "I feel like you want to hear what I have to say; it makes me feel purposeful." This process can occur in most subject areas and at most grade levels. Connecting their own experiences to larger themes in the human story, students begin to realize the thread of purpose and meaning running through their life.

Service Learning and the Search for Meaning and Purpose

When are people going to take responsibility for the state of things? When is it too late? Well—it is too late—what are we going to do about it?

I feel my spirit nourished when I'm helping someone else.

How come there is so much food in the U.S. and the rest of the world, but people are starving?

Many students find meaning through opportunities to contribute to their world. Sheldon Berman (1997), an educator who has devoted much of his work to understanding the development of social responsibility, believes that people must, sooner or later, turn *purpose* into *action*. "Young people are continually negotiating a sense of meaning, place and commitment," writes Berman. "In often subtle ways they ask: Do I have a meaningful place in the social and political world? Are there values that I can make a commitment to and people I can stand with? Am I capable of contributing something useful to others that they will welcome and appreciate?" (p. 28).

Jose, a junior at Choate Rosemary Hall in Connecticut, began to discover answers to these fundamental life questions through his experience in the school's community service program:

> When I go over to the local elementary school to tutor two Spanish-speaking children, they are so excited to see me. I guess they don't get too much attention from a teacher and a classroom that is strictly English-speaking....
>
> When I am with them, I feel special. I am an average student at my school, I don't hold any elected positions, I am not on any varsity team. I do not stand out in any way, and that is OK with me. It is OK with me because for three hours each week, Maria and Miguel make me feel like I am the most important person in the world. It has been really great for us because now the entire class wants to learn some Spanish; we are counting and learning simple phrases. I feel proud to share my heritage, language, and culture with little children (Pashley, personal communication, 1999).

As Jose's essay underscores, school and community service programs give many students an experience of contributing real value to their community. *How* we introduce community service into education, however, is important. "Mandatory volunteerism" programs, which many cities and states in the United States are now legislating, can become so large and impersonal that the system can drain heart and spirit out of the experience. Although such programs often grow out of the intention to build character and good citizenship, educators and policymakers also need to be aware of the potential of such programs for nourishing the spiritual development of youth volunteers—and design the programs accordingly (Kessler, 1999/2000).

Service learning may, indeed, become another "should" in the curriculum, imposing by external command rather than appealing to students' emerging compassion and generosity. "There is no compassion without a sense of wonder and reverence for the mystery of being," writes Abraham Heschel (cited in Gross, 1989). He believes that cultivating character "can only be carried out in depth, as cultivation of total sensitivity" (p. 70).

Mary Pashley (personal communication, 1999), director of community service for Choate Rosemary Hall, inspires her students with the example of Albert Schweitzer (1949), who was keenly aware that service to others is an outpouring of blessing from and to the soul:

> In helpfulness to others, every man can find on his own doorstep adventures for the soul—our surest source of true peace and lifelong satisfaction. . . . In this unselfish labor a blessing falls on both the helper and the helped. . . .
>
> I do not know what your destiny will be, but one thing I do know; the only ones among you who will be really happy are those who have sought and found how to serve. . . .
>
> Without such spiritual adventures the man or woman of today walks in darkness. In the pressures of modern society we tend to lose our individuality. Our craving for creation and self-expression is stifled; true civilization is to that extent retarded.
>
> What is the remedy? No matter how busy one is, any human being can assert his personality by seizing every opportunity for spiritual activity (pp. 1–5).

Giving students the chance to discover how to match their particular passions to the needs of others takes students indirectly to the issue of meaning and purpose. Acknowledging the spiritual dimension more directly can deepen rather than detour their search.

For some students, meaning can come from giving that is not about individual talents or interests, but from expressing their most basic humanity. In activities like packaging and delivering food to the hungry or sitting with a sick child or lonely elder, students experience the simple gifts of being present with an open heart or doing menial labor that will nurture those in need.

As Dayna, a 16-year-old junior, writes:

> I have always volunteered with the Special Populations swim program at our school because of the way I feel afterwards. While I am there in the pool, I forget all about the stresses of my everyday life. . . . I look forward to Thursday evenings as much as the people involved do, I love seeing them smile after they have swam an entire length of the pool, that is something I have always just taken for granted (Pashley, personal communication, 1999).

"Young people cannot develop a sense of their own value unless they have opportunities to be of value to others," write Brendtro and colleagues (1990, p. 26) in *Reclaiming Youth at Risk*. And the behavior of many young people confirms this search for meaning through service. "Contrary to the stereotype of young adults being aloof and devoid of deep convictions," concluded researchers in a recent study of young Americans, "today's young Americans have a strong sense of values and principles, and a well-defined direction for contributing to their community and country" (Hart, 1998, p. 3).

Youth in the 1990s have a profoundly different style in expressing their commitment to service. Although most young Americans of all races engage in community activities, studies show that they are indeed alienated from traditional political and charity-based approaches to social change. Young people seek a more soulful, less institutional approach, where an experience of genuine connection is possible.

A recent example was the "Lilith Fair"—an all-female rock music tour that had charitable fundraising as its main goal. "Think about it," said Sarah McLachlan, the organizing force behind the tour, "Religion is often about feeling like a part of something greater. And music can be a conduit for that." A journalist interviewing the popular singer concludes that it is "this power coupled with the Fair's charitable acts and sense of community that makes the tour a success" (McLachlan, cited in Childerhose, p. 49).

As teachers, we can affirm this soulful dimension of youth culture. Examples of altruism and activism from popular culture can provide a bridge for alienated adolescents to connect with their own yearning for finding meaning through service to others. Instead of judging and distancing ourselves from popular youth culture, we can support this expression of soul in our students by naming and honoring it whenever we see it.

Sheldon Berman (1997) writes: "One of the tasks of adolescence is to find one's own place in the world, to find the intersection of one's personal history with history itself" (p. 62). A service program can respond to the yearning of young people for connection to a larger frame of meaning.

⨯ ⨯ ⨯

A soulful approach to community service can take students beyond "rules" to empathy, beyond fulfilling mandated "service learning" requirements to finding meaning and purpose through giving. Students develop social responsibility not as a burden or obligation, but out of a sense of connection and empowerment. They discover the compassion that makes humans want to alleviate the suffering of others. Through experience, they find that choice and change are possible—first in themselves and, by extension, in the community and society at large.

5

Joy

∞ *Do other people get as overjoyed as I do about little differences and cute things?*

∞ *Why don't I enjoy and appreciate where I am?*

∞ *I want to move many and take joy in every person, every little thing.*

∞ *Do all people have the same capacity to feel joy and sorrow?*

Joy and delight can emerge from the most simple experiences. I recently experienced this "ordinary" joy when my 6-month-old grand-niece chortled with delight as her elders made ridiculous faces and pleasing noises. Gathered for Mother's Day, four generations of our family immersed ourselves in joy as we lost ourselves for nearly a half-hour in the sweet, fresh beauty of this new member of the family.

I don't think I experienced real joy until I was 34 years old. I had certainly felt happiness, satisfaction, contentment, and pleasure. But never before had I felt the power of joy that came over me that winter morning. I was swimming back and forth in an indoor pool with sunlight flooding in through skylights. In the rhythm and solitude of that swim, I floated into a state of consciousness that was new for me. My mind ceased its constant activity. Something new could enter my being.

What entered was joy—a delight and gratitude in being alive. I basked in this new emotion. Then I began to think about how I'd understood the purpose of my life since I was a teenager. The answer I found through those early struggles informed my early adult years. My life would have meaning insofar as I could reduce or eliminate suffering in this world.

I was born to two immigrants in the year they learned that the Holocaust had destroyed much of our immediate family. I was carried

in the womb of that grief. I grew up in a family where suffering was im-
bued with nobility; nobody mentioned joy. Suffering was the reference
point—it was noble both to suffer with integrity and to mitigate the
suffering of others. I became adept at both.

Before that moment in the water, I never thought about joy—not
as an experience, or even a concept or goal. But once it broke through,
it changed my understanding of my existence. I knew that from that
moment on, my life was about discovering and expanding the joy in
my own life and in the people I touch.

As I drove home that morning, a phrase surfaced and repeated over
and over in my mind: "Let it shine, let it shine." In the weeks that followed, the word *spirit* emerged from my mind. I did not know what it
meant, since I had experienced no religious upbringing. Discovering
what that word meant and where it would take me became my search.
My encounter with joy had awakened my spirit.

Hiding Joy

Teenagers seldom talk about joy. Some may not yet have known joy.
Many are more embarrassed to share success than failure, more afraid
to reveal joy than tribulation. Ashamed to feel even moments of joy
when there is so much suffering around them, afraid to stir jealousy in
even those who love them most, adolescents protect their joy as a
well-kept secret. Only when trust grows deep do students share their
joy as easily as they share their pain.

"We're not able to celebrate when life is going great or horrible,"
said Petra when I asked a group of former students why teenagers
didn't talk about joy. "We can't identify with either extreme because
we've been taught to be the same. We edit our emotions so that no one
gets offended. We lose the truth. We lose feelings. We lose who we are."

Another student targeted the competitiveness fostered in school as
a major obstacle to the expression of joy: "You have to separate yourself
from your whole class. There's this big gap between people who do
really well and people who don't. There's rarely any appreciation expressed about other people's accomplishments. I remember when my
friend Celia used to hide her tests, hide her smile, turn over her paper
so we wouldn't know she'd done well."

Students have been raised to feel far more at risk—more vulnerable
and reluctant—in sharing their successes and strengths than in admit-
ting their flaws. Except for the moments of victory on the playing field,
our culture in and out of schools today tends more toward complaint,
criticism, and suffering than toward celebration and joy. "I always

thought you could only get close to people sharing the bad times," remarked a high school student recently, echoing a belief I have heard from teenagers everywhere. So when students first experience the intimacy of "sharing circles," they assume it is primarily a place to share problems.

Many students are also taught not to tempt fate by speaking out loud about good things—"Knock on wood" and other expressions remind us of common superstitions that caution young and old to keep silent about anything really wondrous in our lives. Psychological research has also shown that people are often reluctant to speak about "peak experiences"—the best, happiest, most wonderful moments of one's life—because they are afraid those experiences will be devalued and because it is hard to find words for such moments. Abraham Maslow, who coined the term "peak experience," also believed that people avoided talking about them because they fear acknowledging the sacred dimension of everyday life. "This desacralization," Maslow believed, "can be used as a defense against being flooded by emotion, especially the emotions of humility, reverence, mystery, wonder, and awe" (cited in Davis, Lockwood, & Wright, 1991, p. 87).

In exploring the literature on the spiritual development of students, Weaver and Cotrell's (1992) "urge for enjoyment" is one of the few references to this gateway that I've found. In their schema for encouraging spirituality in the college classroom, they define "the urge to enjoy" as "the desire of the human spirit to experience and express the delight of existence" (James & James, cited in Weaver & Cotrell, 1992, p. 432). They encourage educators to use humor in the classroom and encourage the positive experience of pleasure.

Because students are reluctant to talk about it, I had to search for clues to understand how joy nourished their souls. In virtually every experience of deep connection described by students, I witnessed the expression of joy. I would also see the radiance of joy in their eyes when they talked about what is most important to them in their lives. Certain activities evoked delight in their laugher, voices, and faces. I began to see the variety of experiences that stir this emotion in the souls of young people and the many ways to foster delight inside the classroom:

• Share joyful events and life experiences; remind students that we are here to share our highs as well as our lows.
  • Create celebrations and moments for expressing gratitude.
  • Invite humor.
  • Teach through play.

- Create lessons that awaken the senses and engage the body.
- Foster moments of heartfelt connection within the group.
- Encourage the personal exhilaration and pride that comes when someone takes a new risk or breaks through perceived limitations.

In addition, we can invite students to experience the exultation that comes with the following:

- Taking in or creating art and music.
- Encountering the beauty and majesty of nature.
- Feeling or witnessing the power and grace of the human body in athletics and dance.
- Experiencing or observing the brilliance of the human mind.

Inviting joy into the classroom supports the growth of a storehouse of positive memories from childhood. These memories can mitigate the forces of cynicism, depression, and even despair faced by many youth today. Such memories are "protective factors," promoting resilience throughout life.

Gratitude and Celebration

> I got this little paper American flag on my first trip out of the country. It was a gift from my Latin American hosts. That trip opened my eyes to the developing world and made me appreciate what I have here. It gave me the courage to want to travel more.
>
> —GERALD, age 17

> This photo shows the dog I had when I was little—he's all dressed up here in a tie and hat and glasses. "Waldo" reminds me how much I loved the silliness of childhood, of my simple and carefree life. But this photo also represents how glad I am to be a human being and to be challenged by life's complexities.
>
> —ROGER, age 18

Like many other seniors, Gerald and Roger shared their gratitude through the opportunity to bring in a symbol of what was important to them. Often this gratitude is focused on the simplest, most essential gifts of life. "My spirit is nurtured when I pick cherries," said Lisa, a senior in Oregon.

Most often, I hear this quality of gratitude when students or teachers talk about the joy that comes from giving. They talk of loving and being loved, of blessing others or being honored for who they are.

When I gathered a group of Senior Passage Course alumni to inquire about joy, the dialogue that emerged was about giving to others.

"I was looking for romantic love this year at college; it just wasn't happening," says Todd. "Then I started volunteering at Head Start. I felt that people needed me and in return I needed them. I had gone from a place where I couldn't express love and joy—the academic world—to a world where I could express all my emotions."

"It was at the retreat that I really discovered joy," says Rebecca. "I kept feeling so happy for someone else and that brought joy to me."

"I know what you mean. I felt that way in our group when Cathy was talking about how well things were going for her with Jake. I felt really happy for her, instead of comparing it to my situation. Truly not feeling self-ish, for once, that's what brought me joy."

"I think that's a measure of when you really love someone," says Todd, "when you can step out of your own mood and really support them."

In a similar spirit, students at Choate Rosemary Hall described their experiences of joy in fulfilling their community service requirement. Robby, a 16-year-old sophomore, writes:

> I do not have any younger siblings, so it is fun for me to spend time with Angel, the 8-year-old boy from the local foster home. Angel has led a life that I will never understand.
>
> He has been shuffled from foster family to foster homes most of his life. I have come from a very fortunate, loving, stable family. Yet when we are together, the only thing that matters to Angel is being with me.
>
> He sees things so simply and not with a prejudiced view. He seemed so eager to learn everything I could tell him about the forest as we hiked in a state park. I seem to take a lot for granted; Angel doesn't. He just loved learning about moss growing on trees, he loved comparing the shapes of acorns, and he loved smelling pine needles.
>
> I cannot decipher who was having more joy, Angel learning, or me teaching him (Mary Pashley, personal communication, 1999).

In my work with teachers, I encourage them to remember and share a precious moment from their own childhood so they can have a better understanding of what brings joy into the lives of children. Many teachers express gratitude for moments when they really knew they were loved.

"I remember the Saturday mornings in the park with my father," said Jorge, a huge, lumbering man, with curly brown hair and blue eyes. "He would take me and my brother every Saturday—no matter how tired he was—to the park to fly wooden gliders. He would buy lots of wooden gliders—so when they got stuck up in the trees, there would be more."

For others, it was the experience of being acknowledged that was a precious moment never to be forgotten.

"I remember the day I was elected May Queen in high school," said Karen, a tall woman with red hair. "It was a Catholic school—all girls—and they elected me. I, of course, knew all the bad things I had done. But this honor was an affirmation of my goodness as a person."

For Alejandro, the recognition was much simpler:

> It was the day I was graduating from 6th to 7th grade and my teacher gave me a certificate. It said how well I had done, how good my performance was with Spanish. Having that certificate completely changed the way I looked at school—the way I saw myself at school. From then on, I felt I could succeed, and I went all the way to the top—from all Cs to all As.

Students also express gratitude for being honored.

"Remember how we talked about beauty on the retreat—about finding beauty in yourself and everyone else?" asked Mira. This senior used to carry herself in the way of young people who feel unworthy. "The retreat helped me see I was a beautiful person and that my parents were good people. My parents and I had not been getting along. High school was so hard. In that move from junior high to high school, my self-esteem plummeted.

"Then in senior rites, people would give me compliments, like, I really like your shoes, or you look pretty today. Every time someone did that, I would think about it for days. There had been such an absence of that."

On the other hand, the celebration of a child's beauty by just one parent can be a turning point in that child's life. Savannah was a large African American teacher with an exquisite face. She moved with striking grace in a body so heavy that our culture rarely associates it with beauty.

> I got real heavy when I hit puberty. I remember how Mama would take me shopping and say, "We're going to find you a beautiful dress—a red dress, or a bright green one. We are not buying any of those plain colors for you. None of those somber

tones they're always expecting a big woman to wear. You are a beauty and we shall dress you as one."

This mother had turned a shopping trip from what might have been a painful reckoning into a celebration of her daughter's beauty.

This spirit of celebration can be created for small moments like this in the home and in the classroom. Larger, more traditional forms of celebration can also be enduring sources of joy—when there is a genuine sense of gratitude and communion.

"I want to remember all the Christmases of my childhood when my whole family came together," said Luis, a teacher in the Bronx who grew up in the Dominican Republic. "My aunts and uncles and cousins. Both my grandfathers, both my grandmothers. Maybe I didn't realize it then how special it was. But now, with so many gone—died or moved away—I remember it as such a wonderful time."

Thanksgiving is a natural moment for celebration and gratitude in many classrooms. Because it is a secular holiday,[1] teachers are not usually inhibited by concerns about the law. This can be a wonderful time to invite joy into the classroom. But we need to recall how vulnerable it can be for young people to speak out loud about what brings them joy. We can take special care to make sure the classroom community feels safe before opening this gate. Even so, gratitude on demand may first elicit thoughts of everything the student is *not* grateful for.

When Joy and Sorrow Intersect

Light and shadow. Shadow and light. They go hand in hand, inseparable dimensions of our wholeness. If we focus on joy, images of suffering may rear up and even take over. So often when I ask students or teachers to think of a positive story, several are flooded first with sad memories; when I ask students to think of their gratitude, they can remember only what they want to complain about. This paradox is part of human psychology—naming it for our students can normalize it. They let go of their shame or sense of inadequacy about only thinking of "bad" things in their lives.

Even more effective, especially with children too young to understand the paradox, is to create an activity that welcomes the shadow side first, before we have our Thanksgiving circle on gratitude. Often I ask them to take turns in pairs venting for three minutes each about

---

[1] My colleague Perry Glanzer, at Focus on the Family, reminds me that for many Christians, Thanksgiving is celebrated as a religious holiday with religious origins.

whatever they are *not* grateful for at this moment. The room comes alive when complaint and whining is the assignment. After this release, we can sit in council with hearts open to what we truly appreciate.

One year, with a group of 10th grade students, I suggested we take the first round of council to express what is hard in our life that might get in the way of appreciating what we do have. Our second round would be about giving thanks.

Samantha wants to begin the council. She had been late to class today because she was upset and needs to talk about it. No sooner does she have the "talking stone" than she begins to cry. She sobs: "I had a fight with my best friend last night because I couldn't stand it any longer. We've been friends since 3rd grade, but why does she try to hurt me so much? I got a worse grade than she did on a test yesterday, and she said, 'Yeah, Sam, that's because you're so dumb.'

"I'm not that great in school, and it really hurt me. She's always competing and comparing; and last night when I told her how I felt, she got mad and said I'm always acting stuck-up because I have a boyfriend and I think I'm the greatest. I'm so confused. Am I really acting stuck-up? And what am I supposed to do when my best friend treats me this way?"

After several other students share, Silvie speaks in a half-joking tone about how "lame" her Thanksgivings are because it's just her and her mom and they don't have any family here in Los Angeles and so they usually just go to Sizzler or something. She laughs as she describes how absurdly untraditional their holidays are; then suddenly she becomes very still. Now it's hard for her to speak—she's breathing deeply and looking deep into a dark corner of herself she rarely dares to visit.

Finally, the words come, slowly. "I really miss having a father. It's been so hard for me, not ever having a dad." Two girls flock to each side of her, as she passes the stone to Brandon.

"There's nothing getting in the way of my feeling grateful now," says Brandon, who comes from a strong Christian family, one generation up from the ghetto. "I always feel so thankful for what I have, for my mom and dad, for having enough money to be off the streets and be comfortable."

Now it's Brooke's turn, and she begins by addressing Samantha with words of support and insight. Then she shifts to her own life: "I had a terrible nightmare last night that someone offered me cocaine and I refused to take it—and then they forced it into me. I think it's because I decided two weeks ago to go off pot."

She begins to cry now, and her voice cracks: "It's so hard. I really want to do it, but it's so hard. My friends are really supporting me. Some are even saying they'll go off, too. But then I'm at a party and one of these same kids offers me a joint, and it smells soooo good. I think, this is really good dope. Part of me wants it, and the other part wants to stomp on it and throw it as far as I can hurl it.

"And I tried to talk with my dad about it a couple weeks ago. But he had a bad time with drugs in the '60s; and he said, 'I don't want to hear about this, it scares me.' But I really think I can do it."

When Brook finishes, I speak briefly, interrupting the flow of council. This is the first time I've heard Brooke speak of her drug use, and I feel I must respond: "I'm really proud of you, Brooke, for sharing this with us. I know how hard it is to do this alone, and I think we need to find ways for you to feel supported. I'd like you to stay after class for a few moments so we can make some plans."

John passes the stone without speaking. He always has a hard time waking up for this early morning class. Paul takes it: "My problem's a little like yours, Samantha—it's about a friend. Me and David have been hanging out with this guy; and whenever we kid around at all, he's so sensitive he starts to cry or wants to leave. We don't know what to do. We've really backed off on the teasing—we know he's thin skinned. But even so, he seems to feel we're shutting him out. I really want to be friends with him, but I don't know how."

As I listen, I am still attached to my plan to complete this round and focus the second round on gratitude. But then, all this sharing about troubles with friends leads to an eruption of fear and confusion from one of the last to speak. "My best friend is down to 80 pounds; she hasn't had a period for nine months," says Mandy. She is terrified, angry, guilty, and confused about what to do.

I let go of my plan to focus the second round on gratitude. We put down the talking stone and begin to discuss all the issues, one by one. Problem-solving dialogue takes precedence over joy, and we decide as a group that a small group of girls will go with me to the Dean to discuss their friend's anorexia.

After compassionate problems solving of individual group members' heartfelt concerns, most groups can move into an authentic celebration of positive things. On that day, we found no graceful, upbeat way to end our class before Thanksgiving, but we knew we had done some important work.

Sometimes, it is not during the "complaining" circle that we hear the deepest anguish, but during a statement that is intended to express joy. One of Colleen Conrad's (interview, 1999) students spoke about his love for his grandmother during a discussion of precious moments from childhood. "I was abandoned by my mother, and my grandma took me in," Luis explained, mentioning for the first time to his class this trauma from his early childhood. "My grandma was so loving—she still is—I will always remember how safe she made me feel, how good it was to have her love."

Joy and Humility

We may find joy in celebrating each other's strengths, but there is also an unleashing of joy when we join together in our humility.

Brian was a 10th grade boy who many students considered annoying because of his bravado and macho posturing. We were having a council on fear, preparing for a ropes course retreat. "What were you afraid of when you were little?" I asked them. "And what resources did you call on then or now to deal with your fear?"

In our councils, there is one exception to not speaking when you don't hold the stone. It is a one-syllable expression of support or agreement—like "ho," "yea," or "yes"—that students can offer respectfully when someone has said something that really stirs them.

When Brian talked about his childhood fears, he ended by talking about his teddy bear. Then this 16-year-old soccer star looked around the circle, his eyes wide, and said: "I still use it today, my teddy, when I'm scared or lonely."

Stunned silence was followed by a chorus of four "ho's" from around the circle. We suddenly knew that these boys and girls were not only acknowledging the courage of Brian's risk, but confessing the value of such toys in their own teenage lives. Brian was relieved. For once, he had overcome his aggressive search for approval to tell an embarrassing truth; and it actually brought him more love.

Later, other students recalled that moment as the turning point when that class became a safe haven and intimate community. Joy was palpable in that room when they felt that they could share their frailties, as well as their triumphs.

When we create a safe environment for young people to acknowledge what they have disowned, they begin to forgive themselves and each other. They learn ways to contain and transform destructive emotions such as envy, greed, hatred, prejudice, lust. *"I would like to think that I am not a violent person,"* writes one student anonymously, *"and that I am maybe more gentle, but my mind comes up with all the violent things of death and destruction and I don't know why."* Imagine if the schoolyard killers had been given a safe place for them to verbalize their more frightening emotions without acting on them! We can help our students distinguish between thinking and doing—between impulse and action. Honored for their honesty, supported in their struggle to live with integrity, students are opened to the possibilities for joy.

"Emotions that simmer beneath the threshold of awareness can have a powerful impact on how we perceive and react," writes Daniel Goleman in *Emotional Intelligence*. We begin to have the capacity to evaluate and choose our outlook and behavior only when "that reaction is brought into awareness—once it registers in the cortex" (Goleman, 1995, p. 55).

If, as teachers, we do not have the support or guidance to uncover what lies in our own shadows, we may hurt ourselves or our students. When we uncover what we too have disowned, we become much safer, more responsible teachers. What we do not see in ourselves we may project onto our students and colleagues through feelings of envy or disgust. What we suppress from our own awareness may erupt in ways that are often out of our control.

Many people have confused "thinking positively" with suppressing and disowning the reality of our more difficult emotions and impulses. Although I support training one's mind to affirm life, I am suspicious of those who choose to "smother the other stuff." When we as teachers can acknowledge our own flaws and impulses and embrace the notion that "nothing human is alien to me," we cease shaming our students and greet them with the compassion that allows them to grow, heal, and discover their own ethical core.

As we attempt to invite joy into the classroom, we must always hold these two paradoxes: the coexistence of light and shadow; and the joy that may be intimately associated with pain, fear, or even anger. Perhaps the word "poignant" best captures this quality of joy. Whether it is a piece of music or literature or a story from someone's life, when we describe an experience as poignant, we are talking about the bittersweet pain we feel in our hearts when we are deeply moved.

Awe, Wonder, and Reverence for Life

❧ *What is beauty?*

❧ *Time slipping away has always fascinated me. The constant transformation of moments from future to past through the present is so awe-inspiring and humbling. I am awed by its constant motion, no matter how I split up my day. And I am humbled by my true lack of control over the passage of time.*

❧ *Someone special has come into my life; she is like no other, and that alone is a mystery to me. . . . I feel as though I've tapped into life's biggest wonder—love.*

Closely connected to the spirit of gratitude are feelings of awe, wonder, and reverence for life. A teacher reflected that his own spiritual awakening occurred in a high school physics class when his teacher evoked a sense of awe at the wondrous workings of the universe. Similarly, an English professor in Maine suddenly broke into tears before her colleagues in the freshman support program as she recalled a moment with her late father. "He called me out one evening to stand by his side on the front porch of our home in the countryside. He simply wanted me to share his awe and wonder at the glory of the night sky."

The majesty and intricacies of the natural world are a frequent source of joy for students. The miracle of new life may also be a source of rapture.

"I felt my spirit moving just recently," said Pete, a senior in Oregon, "when I heard my baby's heartbeat for the first time." Pete paused, still holding the rock, and looked around the group for a moment. Sean flashed him a smile. Later Pete told the group about his wedding date two days after graduation and when the baby is due.

"There is no knowledge without reverence," said Abraham Heschel. "For Heschel, education must begin with the development of the individual's ability to wonder, to be amazed at the mystery of being" (Gross, 1989, pp. 60, 70). Before we can become catalysts for joy in the lives of young people, we must reflect on how we adults may actually inhibit our students' experience and expression of awe and wonder. As one senior said:

> There's so much emphasis at my school on knowing. There's no appreciation for curiosity. That's why I think we loved the mystery questions so much; we got to ask questions that people might think were stupid if we asked them in our other classes. I think the most disappointing thing for me in most of high school was that my curiosity wasn't valued. And that's what drives me the most in learning things.

For another student, a 10th grade girl named Cheree, it was her parents, not teachers, who almost cut off her capacity for awe. She told this story in a "check-in" circle about Christmas vacations:

> My parents took us to Hawaii. It was the first time for all of us. I couldn't believe how beautiful it was. There was just one problem. Every time we went to some gorgeous spot, we would get out of the car, my dad would take pictures, and my mom would say, "Okay, let's go. We have a lot of ground to cover here." There was no time to savor anything, to even really see it.

Finally, we came to this place that was called a "sacred site." It was a grove of trees overlooking a bay. There were some ruins there, and I could just feel this place had a story. My mom started to do her "hurry" thing, and I was just sick of it. I can't believe it, but I actually stood up to her. "No, Mom, I'm not getting back in the car. I want to see this place, really be here for a while. What's the point of this trip if we just take a picture and never really have the experience?"

My mom was shocked. And here's the really amazing thing. Later that day, she said to me, "Cheree, you know, you really astonish me sometimes. When you said what you did this morning, it was like you woke me up. Like I'd been sleepwalking through this whole trip. Maybe longer. I know this sounds strange since you're my daughter and you're only 16, but you're my teacher. I really think of you as my teacher sometimes."

Fortunately, Cheree's sense of awe was not stifled. Even more fortunately, this mother had the courage to acknowledge her own shortcomings and honor the wisdom of her child. In moments like this, the awe and wonder deepens—as it is shared and as its power evokes a tectonic shift in the family landscape.

Like the experience of awe and wonder, the state of rapture can come from life's most simple gifts:

"I've loved rainbows all my life," says a high school sophomore. "I had rainbow ribbons for my hair, rainbow sheets for my bed. I got this idea that I wanted to take a picture of a rainbow. I kept taking my camera to soccer practice one week, every day. It was spring. One night, I told my dad about trying to catch a rainbow. The next morning I walked out the front door, and I saw this aspen tree with the most amazing golden light. 'That's not regular light,' I thought, and I looked up and saw this incredible rainbow. I thought it was a rainbow that God gave me."

Radiant joy beamed in her face as she told the story. It mirrored the glow of the tree illumined by the rainbow. Images and memories of light often bring such encounters with joy.

Joyful Release in Rhythm and Movement

The closest I've come to a religious experience has been with music—it was at a concert, and the feeling was maybe like what others mean when they talk about "feeling God." I was so into the music—it carried me somewhere else and filled me with joy. At that moment I felt this peace with life, like I'd come to some height. It was like I could have died right then.

—ALISE, age 17

Time and time again, educators report witnessing waves of joy wash over the faces of young people immersed in the rhythm and repetition of music and dance. Sometimes it is a highly structured, skill-based experience of dance that unleashes the power. When I asked Chip Wood how he first encountered joy in school, he said:

> Oh, I would have to say it was with dance. When I was a principal of a public elementary school, we did a lot of country dancing and circle dancing—and even contradance—with mixed age groups.
>
> Once the kids knew these dances, something quite magical happened. All pretext of difference and posturing dropped away. Such a look of delight came over their faces because they were entirely lost in what they were doing. The universal rhythm that's in our bodies, in our souls—it just takes over (interview, 1999).

Both Wood and I have worked with teachers who have had similar results with introducing a drumming curriculum into the classroom. All children, including those with emotional disabilities, can get lost together as they let go of words and concentrate on the simple, yet riveting, rhythms of syncopation and alternation.

Sometimes the power of rhythm and dance comes in a less structured, more spontaneous form. Working with older students in retreat settings, I have seen the power of drumming and free form dance encourage even serious students to let go into deep nonverbal connection with their inner self and each other.

"My fingers were mine, but acting without my direction," writes one senior in her journal. "As the music intensified, reservations were left behind. When you can play when you think you have no sense of rhythm or dance in a group that's not judging you, that nourishes the spirit. In our jam sessions, everyone is involved. Then you go to prom and see those same people on the outskirts."

For such students, it is not only the rhythm and dance but the spontaneity itself—a wild inventiveness—that stirs their souls and unleashes a current of joy. This capacity and freedom to improvise is essentially the impulse to play.

Play

> Play is older than culture, for culture . . . always presupposed human society, and animals have not waited for man to teach them their playing. . . . They invite one another to play by a certain

ceremoniousness of attitude and gesture. They keep to the rule that you shall not bite, or not bite hard, your brother's ear. They pretend to get terribly angry. And—what is most important—in all these doings they plainly experience tremedous fun and enjoyment (Huizinga, 1996).

In play, our wildness and our humanity can safely meet. Play is the source of much of our learning and a reservoir of creativity. And playfulness is central to childhood: "Children's play is their approach to understanding what's there. In contrast, adults' play is an attempt to retreat from effort," says Margaret Flinsch, founder of one of the first nursery schools in the 1920s ("A Child's Ground of Discovery," 1996, p. 27). When we consider play in the curriculum, we often impose this adult definition that sees it as a retreat from effort, the opposite of work and learning. But, in fact, as Flinsch says, "Play is a trying out—experimenting. . . . Play is exploration, a growing process. . . . In play, there's no time." Particularly for older students who have had to become so serious, the sense of total immersion that often comes with play can transport them into a state of rapture.

As we saw in the stories about rhythm and movement, there is an experience of "losing your self" in play, a timelessness, a stepping out of ordinary concerns that often unleashes the sense of joy. "There are so many restrictions on what you can do and say in school," said a senior in a dialogue about joy. "But in our class, when we got to play like children, making noises, acting crazy, it was amazing. When we don't always have to feel productive, just being allowed to feel that way is so unique." This student, dedicated to achievement in athletics, academics, and service, rediscovered a childlike sense of wonder and joy in the Senior Passage Course. Although most of this course involves serious, highly focused dialogue, the spirit of play weaves in and out of the curriculum.

A teacher in any subject, any grade level can use theater games and adventure games to foster playfulness. James Moffett (1994), in *The Universal Schoolhouse,* describes a variety of board games and card games that add the delight of play to the study of science, math, literature, and social studies. "Games . . . are an ancient folk form of education," writes Moffett. "Before public schooling was instituted, much learning routinely occurred through games passed down from generation to generation" (p. 180). Role-play about serious subjects, a strategy at the heart of social and emotional learning, invites the spirit of playfulness into a classroom by allowing students to step out of ordinary reality, to pretend, to risk new behavior while protected by the mask of illusion. The word "illusion," which frees us to practice new skills in role play, comes from the words "in play."

More generally, we invite playfulness through creating an atmosphere that welcomes spontaneity, laughter, and even silliness and outrageousness. This atmosphere is crucial to tapping the learning potential in play, for games can be facilitated in a spirit of rigidity or emphasis on performance and perfection that denies precisely what can foster resilience in students. "Play is an attitude, a spirit, a way of doing things, whereas a game is a defined activity with rules and a playing field and participants" (Nachmanovitch, 1990, p. 43).

In his book *Free Play: The Power of Improvisation in Life and the Arts,* Stephen Nachmanovitch (1990) refers to play as "the starting place of creativity in the human growth cycle, and one of the great primal life functions. . . . Without play, learning and evolution are impossible. . . . To play is to free ourselves from arbitrary restrictions and expand our field of action. Our play fosters richness of response and adaptive flexibility. This is the evolutionary value of play. . . . Play enables us to rearrange our capacities and our very identity so that they can be used in unforeseen ways" (pp. 42–43). When play emphasizes the freedom to improvise, it develops the capacities for inventiveness and flexibility required to cope effectively with change and challenge.

Remember, however, that for some students and teachers, including myself, improvisational play or adventure learning may not be "fun." Indeed, they may be intimidating and potentially humiliating. Instead of "child's play," *improv* games sometimes feel like a loss of control. Many of my students have delighted in watching their peers do improv but cringe at the suggestion that they join in. Similarly, my first experiences with high ropes courses, alongside my students, evoked intense, leg-shaking fear. So I am not suggesting that play elicits immediate joy for all students or teachers. Acknowledging to our students that some forms of play are hard, rather than fun for some of us, can ease some of the tension and encourage risk taking. Just as some students need permission and respect for not speaking in council, others need permission and respect for opting out of certain games. This is another opportunity to invoke the role of the active observer, or "witness," as a way to preserve dignity for students who choose not to play.

Surprise can be another source of delight. "Children and adults are both helped by shocks, when in a moment one is disarmed from the usual conditioned response," says Flinsch ("A Child's Ground of Discovery," 1996). "At that moment, one is a little freer and more open to what is" (p. 30). Some teachers are masters at the playful art of surprise, at "tricking" their students in a kind and playful way into a state of alertness and readiness to try new ways of doing things.

"Cosmic dates," an activity my students always love, is infused with the sense of surprise and magic. We call them "cosmic" because we draw their names from a bowl two by two to assign them their "date." "You can think of this as random chance, if you like," I tell them. "Or you may consider this to have some meaning—it's up to you to decide or discover." Once they have their partner, they are asked to spend about 15 minutes together, first doing interviews and then just visiting. Here are some interview questions:

- Tell me what you do for fun.
- Tell me what gives you a sense of worth in your life.
- Who loves you, and how do you know they love you?
- Tell me about a change you've experienced.

This activity is most effective on retreats, when there is ample time and a greater spirit of adventure and risk. In modified and abbreviated form, the cosmic dates can be used in class to build connection and trust and to infuse this element of surprise, mystery, and magic to brighten our students' lives.

In a similar spirit, I created a game or ritual for my students, grades 7 through 12, which resembles the fortune cookie tradition. Adding tiny round labels to the bottom of Hershey Kisses, I write positive qualities or virtues on them, such as balance, joy, friendship, peace, solitude, courage, respect, caring, and discipline. I keep the labeled kisses hidden at first. I ask my students to take a moment to reflect on a quality they want to invite into their life in the coming year—an intention they want to set about their own growth. After a few minutes of quiet reflection, I take out the bowl with the candies; and each student takes one. After they look at the quality they receive, we have a council in which they address these questions:

- What is the quality you wanted?
- What is the quality you received on the candy?
- Is there any relationship between these two?

"I asked for love—because my parents are getting a divorce," said one 7th grader. "I wish we could have a little more love in the house. What I got was 'peace,' and I think that it is connected—because I really want the fighting to stop so we can have a little peace in our house."

I often use this game around New Year's to encourage the reflection on goals and intentions that we call resolutions. We can also do more typical goal-setting exercises, but the spirit of play and the element of ritual in this game allow the students to talk about their lives with a new thoughtfulness and depth.

Another game is about awakening the senses. Underlying this game is the trust that we can be *sensual* and still be *sensible*. In a culture that reduces sensuality to sexuality, it is no wonder we deaden our senses to preserve respectful and appropriate behavior. Our senses are a rich reservoir of pleasure and en"joy"ment that are well within the boundaries of respectfulness in schools. In this game, students choose a partner they feel comfortable with. As the teacher leads them through each of the senses, the students are asked to give each other "gifts"of positive sensory images. As Kaley Warner noted in her journal:

> I let him hear rain, the ocean, silence, applause, someone whispering his name.
>
> Then he gave me an apple pie to taste, he let me smell fresh cut grass and hear a perfect chord.
>
> I invited him to smell the ocean, lilacs, fresh baking bread, dinner on the table.
>
> He painted me a scene of a mountain top and a lake with a sunrise, drinking hot chocolate.

This activity must be handled carefully, especially with less mature students, so that it remains constructive and builds trust, rather than undermining it.

When play becomes essential in our pedagogy, we help our students learn to distinguish laughter and playfulness from disrespect or rudeness. They learn how to balance and integrate seriousness with playfulness, rather than regarding them as contradictory. And they appreciate that serious lessons can be learned in a manner that is playful and fun.

An ally that brings joy throughout the curriculum, play becomes essential for educators who choose to emphasize creativity—the subject of our next chapter.

6 *Creativity*

❧ *Why can I be so inspired at one moment and then be so completely uninspired?*

❧ *How can I be more imaginative?*

> There is something that happens to me in pottery class—I lose myself in the feeling of wet clay rolling smoothly under my hands as the wheel spins. I have it last period, so no matter how difficult the day was, pottery makes every day a good day. It's almost magical.
>
> —CAROL, high school senior

As I began writing this book, I wondered whether creativity is indeed a gateway to the soul of students. In all my years of working with young people, students rarely mentioned it. At the same time, I saw that creative expression—particularly in the arts—is perhaps the most familiar way educators think of nourishing the spirit in school. One can easily grasp the connection between artistic expression and soul; this connection appears safely "nonreligious" and therefore easy to justify including in the classroom. Although our beliefs certainly differ about the *source* of creative inspiration—God, the muse, the collective unconscious, the complexity of each person's inner being—most of us have had some *experience* of being connected to the spirit through creative expression.

I have felt this connection. When my 7th grade students do improvisation or ask to perform a dance routine for the class, or when I attend the talent show at the local high school with my son, I see the other students more passionately engaged, more wildly enthusiastic about the original work of their peers than for almost any other kind of performance.

But if creativity is a gateway to the soul of students, why didn't my students talk about it?

I began to search actively for clues. I asked former students, interviewed colleagues I perceived to be especially creative teachers, arranged to go into classrooms and ask students directly to speak about this subject. Young and old reminded me that creativity replenishes the soul not only through the arts, but also in the way we meet challenges in every domain of the curriculum and of life.

I found many inspiring stories by young people who were deeply moved, and even profoundly changed, through an encounter with artistic expression or with an ingenious solution to thorny problems. I listened to teachers from different disciplines and grade levels who are passionately committed to stirring the creative drive and have found successful methods for doing so.

I also heard from many students and teachers an angry or resigned indictment of an educational system that they believe has stifled, not nourished, creativity. Listening to their stories of how creativity has been banished from the curriculum, I understood my students' silence.

Creativity in Exile

> I used to be creative in elementary school. Now I'm always trying to please my parents—they're brilliant and they expect me to be. There isn't time for me to be creative. I really miss it.
>
> —KATHYRN, 8th grade

> When you're younger, you have the time to make up games and be creative. As you get older, we have more work, not enough time, and when you do have it, you don't have the energy or you've forgotten because it's been so many years since we were creative.
>
> —WILL, 9th grade

Students and teachers alike lament the shift in priorities that occurs after elementary school—a shift that diminishes the opportunity for creative expression.

Let's look first at the arts in education. Students and educators have observed not only a devaluation of the arts, but also an ethos in which the arts curriculum is devoid of an invitation to genuine creative expression. Joy Guarino (interview, 1999), a specialist who offers movement classes to help students work with their feelings, laments the elimination of creativity from much arts education:

> What gets confusing in the schools is that even when the arts are taught, creativity is not a part of it. The curriculum becomes the important thing, and the child's creativity is not important. It happens all the way from preschool to college. Let's say kids are cutting out shapes to make penguins. I see two kinds of teaching—one where the teacher is very clear about the shapes and how they should fit together. Another where the teacher says, we're going to make penguins, do it however you want to.

> I really don't know what's supposed to be taught: the skills with scissors or the imagination. Most teachers in schools have such preconceived ideas about what art is supposed to be and what it's supposed to look like. There's no room for kids to follow their own passion.

To the degree that the arts do have the power to invite creative expression, we *still* face their banishment from the curriculum as time and funds go to academic coursework.

Doug Eaton (interview, 1999) saw this trend in his school and decided that, in his own high school science classroom, he could make a difference. "Our school has one art teacher, a half time choir and band instructor, one industrial arts teacher and one home economics teacher for 1,200 kids," says Eaton. "I began to see that many of our students could never have these experiences with creative self-expression. Art and science make a fine marriage. I enjoy integrating things that draw upon spirit and creativity."

Eaton uses drawing to teach observation skills; finger painting to begin to evoke students' preconceptions about the ocean; and when they study Australian wildlife, his students make didgeridoos out of PVC pipe. "Oh, the sounds we get out of them!"

The devaluation of creativity in schools is manifest not only through marginalizing, eliminating, and objectifying the arts. As storyteller Laura Simms illustrates in the following account, creativity is a way of thinking, learning, and expressing oneself that goes beyond the arts into the entire way we understand and relate to the world.

> There was a little girl whose father died on the second day of a five-day storytelling residency I did at an elementary school. I was told she'd been sent home, and I didn't expect her to come back.

> But she came back the next day and was there the rest of the week. Each day, she sat back and didn't participate; but she listened to the stories intensely.

At the end, when I was leaving the school, she caught my sleeve
on the steps. Speaking out in her childish voice, she said to me: "I
liked your class. Every night I went home and I put my father in
all the stories. And I thought about life and about death. Thank
you." She was not more than 7 years old. That's creative living
(interview, 1999).

Grief, violence, science, math, conflict resolution—solving the
problems of daily life all become the playground, the laboratory for a
creative response. And for many students and educators, messages and
methods of our current pedagogy suppress rather than stimulate creative solutions.

"So much of our education involves theories about society or nature that have already been preformed," says Columbia Teachers College professor Doug Sloan (interview, 1999). "So the student is
supposed to learn the theories and then apply them to the world. That
allows the student only to manipulate the world, not to actually know
the world. There is no listening in that."

This narrowing in schools of our definitions of intelligence and our
repertoire for teaching and learning, writes Robert Sternberg (1997),
turns education into "a closed system" in which students are "taught
and assessed in ways that emphasize memory and analysis." Creativity,
concludes Sternberg, goes "unappreciated and unrecognized, . . . simply not considered relevant to conventional education" (p. 20).

Creating the climate and the skills for fostering creativity is essential to educating a generation of young people who can visualize new
solutions to the problems of today and tomorrow's work force, social
fabric, and environment. To these practical rationales for honoring the
creative drive, I want to add the call from the soul. An 8th grade girl
best captures this connection: "Creativity is an outreach of your spirit
into form," she said. "Then, you can see it, hear, feel, touch it."

But what is this creativity that feeds the soul or expresses the spirit?
Is it a process or a particular kind of product? This chapter explores the
qualities of both process and product and suggests practices and principles that allow creativity to flourish in the classroom. The chapter also
examines some difficult feelings that may arise in both students and
teachers when creativity is unleashed and suggests constructive ways
to respond.

Definitions of Creativity: Product and Process

> I was in a painting class. It was the first time I did a painting just from my mind—an image I created in my mind. It was not a representation. It was completely from the depths of my mind.
>
> It worked! I found the colors, the images I needed to represent this feeling I had inside me. This is me, this painting. I made it—nobody else could have done this. It's like physical proof of me.
>
> —JULIA, college freshman, New York

For Julia, the outcome of her creativity was clearly crucial to the meaning and joy it brought to her soul. We can view creativity in terms of both the quality of the outcome and the nature of the process. Let's look first at the outcome. Whether I am listening to 8th grade students brainstorming about the word *creativity,* or reading the vast literature on this subject, the product of creativity is often defined by words such as *newness, authentically expressive, inventive* and *imaginative.*

Julia's product was a piece of art. In other chapters, we have seen creative outcomes in a response to a problem, whether it is from a student or group of students or a teacher: How do we stand up for our positions on war without demonizing those who hold other positions? How do we bring a weak and dying girl to our closing ceremony? In each case, what made these moments moving was the unforeseeable burst of creativity that solved the problem in a new way.

Doug Sloan (1994) refers to the "experience of genuine newness" as one of his primary definitions of nourishing spirit through education. This encounter with what is genuinely new and fresh is what Sloan sees as deeply satisfying to the spirit. "A new insight, a new beginning, a new possibility, a new hope—the breaking in of newness in all its forms—this is often our most compelling experience of spirit" (p. 13).

Encountering what is fresh and original is certainly a clue to the experience of creativity, but novelty is not a sufficient definition. What is the source of genuine newness that distinguishes creativity from novelty?

This type of *outcome,* where the old and familiar has been dissolved and reconfigured into new patterns, emerges from a *process* that extensive research agrees involves a sequence of stages: preparation, incubation, inspiration or illumination, and verification[1] (Storr, 1965, p. 261).

---

[1] I have come across variations on this stage theory in at least half a dozen sources. Another variation is "preparation, incubation, discovery, elaboration, and validation" (Gardner, 1993, p. 392).

Knowing the natural rhythm of the creative process, educators can foster creativity by what we convey to our students about timing and about dealing with ambiguity, uncertainty, mistakes, and getting stuck.

The Process of Creativity: Steps and Stages

As with all stage theories, we cannot expect each person to follow every step and move in exactly the same sequence. Essential to this sequence is the dynamic interplay of focused attention and diffuse awareness, effort and receptivity, varying activities that open the door to genuine creativity.

Preparation

In preparation, we gather skills, principles, and data. We thoroughly investigate the problem through every lens of perception and every mental model we can access. It is a time of focus and discipline, when we often benefit from the rational, conceptual mind. Traditional schooling emphasizes these skills.

Incubation

Incubation, on the other hand, requires us to let go. To stop trying. To stop doing. Incubation is the "sleep on it" phase when we benefit from diffuse awareness, receptivity, and patience to wait while nothing is happening. As early as the 1930s, John Dewey described this process in detail:

> After prolonged preoccupation with an intellectual topic, the mind ceases to function readily. It apparently has got into a rut; the "wheels go around" in the head, but they do not turn out any fresh grist. . . . This condition is a warning to turn, as far as conscious attention and reflection are concerned, to something else. Then, after the mind has ceased to be intent on the problem, and consciousness has relaxed its strain, a period of incubation sets in. Material rearranges itself; facts and principles fall into place; what was confused becomes bright and clear; and mixed-up becomes orderly, often to such an extent that the problem is essentially solved (p. 284).

Dewey not only appreciated the role of going fallow as essential to a creative discovery or synthesis, but he went on to explain the dynamic relationship of this phase to the earlier phase of *preparation* and the phase of *verification* that will be required in the end:

> But this bringing forth of inventions, solutions, and discoveries rarely occurs except to a mind that has previously steeped itself consciously in material relating to its question, has turned matters over and over, weighed pros and cons. Incubation, in short, is one phase of a rhythmic process (p. 284).

The incubation phase, which has perhaps had the most attention in the literature on creativity, is also the most alien to the environment of schools and least understood and valued in our culture. We have confused receptivity with passivity, waiting with doing nothing. If we can give our students the tools to actively court a receptive state, we open the door to incubation.

When we cultivate in the classroom the silence, stillness, and solitude suggested in Chapter 3, we are providing the opportunity and building the "muscles" for incubation. For some students, incubation may also involve a certain chaos, or playfulness, to unhinge the "doing" mind long enough for something new to break through. Incubation may take seconds, minutes, a quick nap or a night's sleep, a month, a year, or more.

Illumination or Inspiration

Illumination comes into the empty, receptive womb or the freewheeling playfulness of incubation. The seed blossoms. Or a new synthesis appears. People differ on the source of this inspiration; but whatever its source, inspiration arrives. Imaginative and intuitive minds are crucial here—but often in a marriage to the skills, principles, and forms cultivated in the preparation stage. Now comes the creation—an authentic expression that has meaning for a particular person at that moment in response to a particular context.

Neville (1989) notes that metaphor is often useful in triggering illumination: "'What is it like?' is a question that can break us open into non-verbal modes of expression that may provide clues to a new insight or invention." Neville also warns us that "evaluation inhibits the illuminative phase" (pp. 175, 176). Although assessment and feedback may be crucial to genuine creativity in the verification phase, they may short-circuit the freewheeling expression essential to discovering something new.

Mary Lou Faddick (interview, 1999), founder and director of Foothills Academy in Wheatridge, Colorado, describes the moment when she saw a student move through a long incubation to a startling illumination:

> It's so often hard to see the incubation process in our students. They don't really know how to talk about it, so we don't hear much about it. But I watched it happening once.
>
> Maria was a blind girl—a very intelligent student in my writing class. She had great ideas, but they were all very linear. Poetry was frustrating for her. One day, four or five months into this creative writing class, she began to giggle. Suddenly she was coming up with images that tickled her.
>
> Do you know what she would say? "I see it; I see it!"
>
> In her imagination, she did see it. This little girl was writing in braille; and, honestly, these images were so beautiful—each like a little gem.
>
> After this, she started writing songs with her mother, who is a musician. It was startling for me to watch: The process was clear to see. The incubation was long and frustrating, but when the illumination came, her images came from a deep sensual experience.

This story captures the "aha" moment commonly used to describe illumination.

Verification

The last stage, verification, comes when we hone and polish our inspiration. We check against our efforts in our "preparation" to refine the product—whether it's a song, a sculpture, or a solution to a problem in math, science, or community conflict. Have we yet completed the most thorough, elegant, or responsive piece of work? In many instances, constructive feedback and the opportunity to refine in response to verification allow completion of the creative cycle.

Welcoming Creativity

Understanding the steps and stages of the creative process can certainly empower teachers to allow a natural unfolding that will nurture creative expression. Here are four other principles that can help us welcome creativity and infuse it into our approach to teaching and learning:

- Be open to the unknown and unexpected.
- Bridge differences—in culture, beliefs, and ways of knowing.
- Dance the paradox of form and freedom.
- Hold the tension between safety and risk.

Being Open to the Unknown

> Surprise is an experience that plays a part at the birth of an idea
> and during the work itself. . . . Open-mindedness, flexibility, will-
> ingness to trust hunches, and *curiosity* are factors that emerge re-
> peatedly as facilitating and favoring creativity.

> —HOWARD GARDNER (1993, p. 382)

A willingness to be open to surprise and accidents, to the experience of mystery and not knowing where the process is going, is familiar
to people who have succeeded in unleashing their own creative power.
In a 1999 interview, Linda Lantieri, coauthor of *Waging Peace in Our
Schools* (1996), recalls such a moment from her second year of teaching:

> It was the week before Thanksgiving. I wanted to offer an experi-
> ence in the classroom where young people could create a gift
> they would give their families for Thanksgiving. It was a creative
> writing project. I was encouraging them to think of something
> they were grateful for—an object, a quality in nature, a person.
> Then they would write a letter to it: like, "Dear Chalk," or "Dear
> Sunshine," or "Dear Roller Skate." We would assemble all these
> letters into books they could bind and decorate and take home to
> their families.
>
> I started that first step with a brainstorming activity of all the
> things that make us feel happy. We were going around, with chil-
> dren speaking of objects and people they cherished until a boy in
> the front row raised his hand and said, "I'll tell you what I'm *not*
> thankful for—I'm not thankful for the drug dealers on 103rd
> Street."
>
> Another boy called out, "And I'm not thankful for all that trash
> that's all over the street and not in the bins or the garbage
> trucks."
>
> By the time the third child spoke, I was drawing a line down the
> middle of the blackboard with "thanks" on one side and "no
> thanks" on the other.
>
> A powerful book of their letters came out of that experience, with
> most of the students talking about the inequalities they saw in
> their world. To get to that beautiful expression in my students, I
> had to allow their creativity to stretch beyond my limits of what I
> thought this project was going to be.
>
> If I had maintained that box of my original idea of gratitude, we
> would have missed the very preciousness of what actually hap-

pened. The depth of that final gift they made for their families was so much more real and honest.

As teachers, we often prove our competence and responsibility by good "planning." But our own creativity—and the creativity of our students—may be at odds with even the best of plans. By "allowing" the process, rather than steering and restricting ideas to her original design, Lantieri both expressed her creativity as a teacher and opened the way for inspiration in her students. How many of us close down immediately when our plan appears to be thwarted, by reminding our students what we're "supposed to be doing now?" By valuing openness and being willing to be surprised, we can override this reaction and discover a more creative response.

We can teach students the practice of observation to help them awaken this quality of open engagement. Doug Eaton (interview, 1999) cultivates observation early in the semester when he has students observe a leaf through drawing each detail that they see without ever looking at their paper. "The outcome sometimes amazes the kids," says Eaton. "In my biology class, I often hear 'I am not an artist; I can't draw.' We see the way that drawing skills come from observational skills."

Karen Halverson (personal communication, 1999), teaching at the American International School of Mozambique, describes a similar approach with a 3rd grade class:

> We needed some inspiration beyond what our classroom walls and school playground could offer. We were writing poetry and decided to head down the road to the ocean. We sat down on the sand; and I read a few poems about nature, the ocean, about truly seeing. Then students set off, notebook and pencil in hand, for a time of silence and solitude, a time to see and to write. After a while, the hermit crabs, jellyfish, shells, and playfulness of the ocean were just too much to resist any longer. . . . Students put their writing aside and set out to explore. I watched the students connect to the nature around them and to each other, fully present in the moment the sand and sea was offering to them. Back in the classroom, students shared the pieces they had written.
>
> I was awed by the pureness of their words, what they had truly seen and experienced out there by the sea. These were not poems to be revised—these were pure expressions of the soul.

For these educators, this quality of being "fully present" to something outside of ourselves allows creativity to be reborn.

Another aspect of staying open to the unknown is the quality of *immersion.* Immersion means getting lost in what we are doing—losing track of time, losing concern about outcome. "Art enables us to find ourselves and lose ourselves at the same time,"observed Thomas Merton (1955, p. 34). In immersion, we lose control without losing competence; something else seems to be steering the ship.

Movement teacher Joy Guarino (interview, 1999) describes the challenges of helping students discover immersion. "So many adolescents just 'freeze up,'" says Guarino. "'Just tell me what you want,' they ask the teacher. They can't let go." But in so many of her stories, an important transformation occurred when a student finally immersed himself in the creative experience. "One boy was just fooling around with a big dry mop—he moved that handle and swung it around a lot and then began to turn it into a movement study about how hard he's had to work in his life to get to where he is now. He just let himself go."

Karen Halverson (personal communication, 1999) writes about a 3rd grade student in Mozambique:

> Her whole body was completely, fully in the moment of her creation, working with pastels to respond to the life and work of Georgia O'Keefe.

> Her arms moving with each stroke of her chalks, her hands intensely brushing and blending the colors. The act of creation is opening and unleashing something that lies within. Although in the midst of 13 other people, Lena is entirely alone, pouring her self in color onto paper. When she finishes, she steps back and sees. "Aaaaah"—joy shines on her face, the joy of creating from within.

This practice of staying open while listening and looking is at the heart of this book. For students, the "council" process creates the discipline of listening attentively while suspending judgment and deferring reaction. In "discovering" others—and their differences—through focused listening, students invent new possibilites for themselves. As teachers, we stay open to our students' questions and insights—and even creatively revise our lesson plans in response. Teachers and students may also discover that apparently unbridgeable differences can be the source of creative breakthrough.

Bridging Differences

A bridge is a structure that provides passage over a gap or barrier. As teachers, what is the attitude we model when we enter a gap or encounter a barrier? Do we see it as an *either–or* choice? A hierarchy of *better* and *worse*? Or do we consider how we might create a bridge to span and connect once divided realms?

"The essential creative perception is concerned with linking situations or ideas which have hitherto been conceived as incompatible; in other words, with forming new unions between opposites," writes Anthony Storr (1965), summarizing the insights of Arthur Koestler. "In science, a new hypothesis characteristically reconciles and supersedes previously incompatible hypotheses. In the arts, balance and contrast between opposites is usually an essential part of creating an aesthetic pattern" (p. 201).

When differences seem irreconcilable—whether different views, cultures, or ways of knowing and learning—we can easily become stuck and divisive. "But differences can be catalysts for changes, creativity, and new ways of doing things," says Pamela Moore (1996, pp. 22–25), a specialist in antibias education. Moore highlights our choice in how we teach about similarity and differences. In the multicultural approach to education, she sees an opportunity for catalyzing growth both through *connection*—sharing what groups have in common—and through facing the *challenge* of differences with an openness to new possibility.

Linda Lantieri (interview, 1999) describes a moment of creative breakthrough in a diversity workshop with a group of middle school students.

> The group had worked hard to come together, and you could feel it happening. Then Lisa, a Korean American girl, told us a story of what happened to her when she was 8 years old. She was on a train platform; out of nowhere came four young black men who approached her and almost pushed her into the tracks. "And to this day, I have never touched a black person," she said, and started to cry.
>
> One of the African American boys in our group raised his hand. "Do you think that this might be the moment that you can do that?" he asked. He held his hand out there shaking. "You can touch me." She got up, walked across the room and took it.

"Can you imagine the courage that boy had?" recalls Lantieri with amazement. "Because of him, long-held stereotypes are beginning to dissolve in front of us." Such breakthroughs become possible only in a climate that supports both honesty and possibility, safety and risk.

Integrating Ways of Knowing

What are the creative possibilities inherent in different styles of knowing and learning? If we become stuck in one mode—whether the physical, feeling, or conceptual way of knowing—a creative response is unlikely. In a 1999 interview, Doug Sloan cites the careful cultivation and integration of these three modes in Waldorf education—a curriculum known for it emphasis on creative expression.

The Physical Way of Knowing. Sloan sees the first way of knowing—the physical—as the foundation for creativity. This kind of knowing involves entering right in to the experience and making it your own:

> What all scientists draw on in their laboratory is this deep knowing that goes into our bodies. It provides the background and context that enables us to make connections. For a creative response, our ideas must be grounded in real, lived experience, not just in formal, abstract conceptions (interview, 1999).

In Waldorf education, this embodied way of knowing is awakened for children under age 7 by encouraging movement as part of everything that is learned. When they learn to count, they move and clap their hands. "When learning to draw, the child uses large block crayons so that the color can almost be felt as the child draws" (Miller, J., 1999, p. 76).

Much of U.S. education, however, neglects this physical way of knowing that is developmentally most appropriate to very young children. Young children spend long hours with television and computers that never engage their bodies. "If the physical way of knowing doesn't come first or is shortchanged," says Sloan in his 1999 interview, "children never develop that sense of confidence of being at home in the world that is a prerequisite for creativity."

The emphasis on cognitive learning at the expense of all other modes of learning has led to a movement to eliminate recess and build schools without playgrounds. Sloan voices alarm at this trend: "All the mainstream research supports the importance of play to that physical way of knowing, which is critical for later intellectual development." Not only creativity, but cognitive development itself is jeopardized when the early need for embodied learning is neglected.

The Feeling Way of Knowing. The second stage of knowing and learning in the Waldorf philosophy comes through *feeling*. Sloan (1999) describes how this mode is also critical to both creative and conceptual thinking: "Relationship, sounds, color, other people—that too is a kind of lived knowledge which makes possible ideas later on that are full of life and power. Ideas that are not just abstract but also grounded in *caring* for the world."

In addition to the physical and feeling ways of knowing, Howard Gardner (1993) reminds us of two other ways of knowing that contribute to creativity—intuition and the unconscious:

> In science, mathematics, and the arts, there is widespread recognition of the significant place occupied by intuition, unconscious promptings, inexplicable insights, and the sudden awareness of relationships. Scientific discovery and artistic creations are hardly the result solely of rational considerations (p. 390).

Imagination: Another Way of Knowing. No discussion of creativity or soul would be complete without mentioning another way of knowing—the imagination. Where would invention be without imagination? If we could not imagine the unknown, how could new solutions or artistic expressions come into form?

Like the body, imagination is jeopardized in growing children by television and video games. The fast, easy, intense flood of images displaces the child's own urge to create personal images. And the pace of entertainment and activity leaves little time for the imagination.

We have already discussed the role of silence and aimlessness in making room for the imagination. We have seen how play, particularly improvisation, can startle the imagination awake. In addition to silence and play, educators committed to fostering creativity have mentioned five other tools for awakening the imagination: metaphor, symbols, images of nature, ritual, and open-ended questions. Each of these tools creates a gap—whether it is between one sense and another, between the ordinary and extraordinary, between human and other, or between the familiar and the mysterious. Imagination is the bridge we access to cross those gaps.

Creativity flourishes most often as a synthesis or integration of many modes of knowing—left brain/right brain; reason and intuition; imagination and observation; and physical, emotional and conceptual ways of knowing.

In our educational system, disconnection has often been the response to difference. Our creativity can help bridge the unbridgeable when we accommodate differing learning styles, listen to divergent thinking, and are tolerant of cultural distinctions. In the way we model our own approach to difference and the opportunities we provide, we can activate our students' creative response.

Dancing the Paradox of Form and Freedom

> I express my creativity in athletics. I know that sounds strange, but it's true. Like in basketball, I hate it when we have to run set plays. It's so boring. But when I get to be creative, to make the passes I think I should make, then I get excited. And the more excited and involved I get, the more creative I am.
>
> —WILL, 8th grade student

Once we hold ourselves open to differences, we enter the territory of paradox. In paradox, we hold two beliefs that are not only different, but apparently contradictory in nature. The gift of paradox, used wisely, is that we may indeed have both. In encouraging creativity in the classroom, I have encountered two crucial contradictions: the paradox of form and freedom and the paradox of safety and risk.

The educators we have met in this book differ about the relative importance and proper balance of form and freedom in nourishing creativity. Some stress structure, particularly in the preparation stage. Without structure, they believe that students will flounder. Others believe that too much structure, too soon, can douse the creative spark.

"Poetry is one way that I encourage a great deal of creativity. My philosophy in 8th grade is that form—rhyme scheme, meter, etc.— can be taught later," says Colleen Conrad (interview, 1999). "At this age, the important task is to give students a voice and to help each one realize he or she has valuable stories to tell." Conrad immerses her students in poetry from many cultures. For this teacher, freedom takes priority over form.

Chip Wood (interview, 1999) takes a different approach to teaching poetry. "Often people don't put enough structure when teaching creativity. They do the structure with academics and then with creativity, they tell their students, just 'paint' or 'write.' You don't get much creativity because the kids are lost." Wood moves slowly, providing what he calls "scales," where student practice poetic forms without a lot of expectations.

Like Wood, Lantieri (interview, 1999) believes it is crucial to provide the forms—the "toolkit"—students can draw on to use creatively in response to any particular situation. "It's not that there's a prescription of how you might deal with every conflict. We provide a set of skills, as well as some underlying principles of nonviolence that you can draw on to respond in a creative way," says Lantieri, national director of the Resolving Conflict Creatively Program.

One of Lantieri's most powerful examples of this creative response is about the day violent youth threatened her own life. Early one morning, she was suddenly surrounded by three young men on a desolate street in Harlem. "One of the boys reached into his pocket and took out a knife with a shiny four-inch blade. As all three pressed closer to me, the young man with the knife said, 'Give me your purse. Now.'"

Although Lantieri felt terrified, she used the tools she had learned for remaining calm:

> "I'm feeling a little uncomfortable. You know, guys, you're a little into my space. I'm wondering if you could step back a little bit?" I waited cautiously. I glanced down and was shocked to see three sets of sneakers take three steps back. "Thank you," I said. "Now I want to hear what you just said to me, but to tell you the truth, I'm a little nervous about that knife. I'm wondering if you could put that away?"

> I waited for what felt like an eternity and then watched the knife slip into a pocket. The boys and I were working it out.

> I quickly reached into my purse and took out a $20 bill, realizing that this was no time to ignore such a request. I was glad I had it. But how to stay neutral—not take sides?—was what went racing through my mind. I caught the eye of the young man with the knife in his pocket and asked, "Who should I give it to?" "Me," was his response. I looked over at the other two guys and asked if they were in agreement. One of them said, "We could cash it at the corner at the *bodega*." My God, I thought, we're actually problem-solving together.

> "Great," I said, as I handed the first boy my twenty. I focused on all three and said, "Now here's what's going to happen. I'm going to stay right here while you walk away." They looked quite puzzled. The script had changed. Without a word, they started to slowly walk away, glancing back at me as I managed to keep my two feet firmly planted, although my knees began to quiver (Lantieri & Patti, 1996, pp. 60–61).

What allowed her creativity to bloom in that moment, Lantieri emphasized in a later interview in 1999, were the skills and principles she had learned: "I brought to that situation a foundation, a principle of knowing that when these boys are coming toward me, making violent gestures, that if my next move is violent, I will escalate the danger."

Lantieri and Patti (1996) suggest regular opportunities for students to practice the skills in the problem-solving "toolkit." "One of the best means of involving young people in decision-making processes is through regularly scheduled class meetings in which young people problem-solve about class issues" (p. 45). Like learning to type or play tennis or drive a car, the more the forms become habituated through this regular reinforcement, the more freedom there is for the creative spirit. Recalling the stages of the creative process, we can see that a disciplined attention to form is part of the preparation that precedes the inspiration for creative expression.

For Conrad, form and discipline are more important later, in the verification phase of discovering a new creative capacity. Conrad's students are so riddled with self-doubt and alienation that when she wants to inspire in them a love for poetry, she believes that too much form too early would scare them away.

Each teacher works with the dynamic tension between form and freedom in stimulating creative expression or problem-solving. The particular balance will vary with the task, the group, and even the mood on a given day. The goal is not to choose one or the other or even a static balance. Creativity flourishes when we hold the tension and make choices that are fluid and responsive to the reality we face.

Holding the Tension Between Safety and Risk

> Creativity is a risk. You're afraid to take that part of you and put it out where people can judge you. Your creativity is you, it's a part of you; and when they judge you it really hurts.
>
> —SARAH, 8th grade student

> I feel more comfortable at home, but not more creative. I'm more creative at school.
>
> —PAUL, 9th grade student

Safety and Risk. Creativity often involves a sense of danger. As Sarah, in the preceding quote, wisely claims, "creativity is a risk." Putting things together in a new way or expressing yourself involves exposure, vulnerability. "Research suggests that highly creative people make more mistakes than their less imaginative peers. . . . In creative problem-solving a mistake is an experiment to learn from, valuable information about what to try next" (Goleman, Kaufman, & Ray, 1992, p. 43). To be able to take these risks—to explore, make mistakes, and wander "out of the box"—students need to feel safe.

Teachers are more likely to provide a climate for creativity when they feel that it is safe to take risks. When our school went through an accreditation process, teachers were asked to evaluate whether they felt their departments encouraged divergent thinking. A gifted new teacher (personal communication, 1990) wrote about the climate in our team that allowed her to be creative:

> I am able to think in varied ways, to experiment and make mistakes, to explore *all* angles, when, and only when I feel loved, respected, safe, appreciated, seen for my strengths and understood in my weaknesses. . . . Not being judged or coldly examined, being allowed to believe there is more than *one* path to any given destination—being unafraid to argue, to disagree with an authority figure, also encourages me to think divergently.

But safety is not to be confused with comfort. Prolonged comfort can easily dampen the fire of creativity. Some kind of challenge, problem, or tension is often the stimulus for creativity. Even profound fear, as in Lantieri's story, can be a stimulus to creativity when the foundation for a constructive response is present. Safety seems to be the *opposite* of risk, but is often a *precondition* for risk. The balance of these apparently contradictory conditions varies with each person and each situation.

Relaxed Alertness. This book has emphasized the importance of creating a safe environment if we want to encourage authentic expression in the classroom. In an interview for *Educational Leadership* (Pool, 1997), Renate Nummela Caine explains the basis for this principle in terms of brain function:

> When we feel threatened, we downshift our thinking. Downshifted people feel helpless; they don't look at possibilities; they don't feel safe to take risks or challenge old ideas. . . .
>
> The system of traditional education can be a threat that inhibits higher levels of learning. If as a teacher I am in charge of the curriculum, you as the student are supposed to learn what I say you must learn. I know the answers that you have to get. I'm also going to tell you how long it will take you to learn this and when it's due. And not only that—I evaluate you and your work. . . .
>
> Students are doing what teachers want them to do. And downshifted people can do some things well, like memorizing, because the brain perseverates under threat and likes to do things over and over again—repetition provides a sense of safety when you feel helpless. . . .
>
> But real thinking—making connections, higher-order think- ing, and creativity—is incompatible with that kind of environment (p. 12).

Caine uses the term *relaxed alertness* to describe the ideal state for critical thinking. This same principle, "low threat, high challenge," can be applied to creativity as well. "For making connections and actually changing their thinking on the basis of accrued knowledge, they need relaxed alertness—that is, safety and challenging learning experiences" (Pool, 1997, p. 13).

Criticism—and Support. "When they judge you, it really hurts," says the young adolescent in the earlier quote, echoing the sentiments of most of her peers, who agreed that the decline of creativity after elementary school was directly related to the fear of being criticized and mocked. As we saw earlier, there can be a constructive role for feedback and criticism in the "verification" stage of creativity. But the safety that invites creativity in its early stages usually requires suspending judgment.

In his study of highly creative individuals, Howard Gardner (1993) discovered that creativity is often stifled if critique comes too early in the creative process: "Knowledge that one will be judged on some criterion of 'creativeness' or 'originality' tends to narrow the scope of what one can produce (leading to products that are then judged as relatively conventional); in contrast, the absence of an evaluation seems to liberate creativity" (p. 25).

It is not only the absence of criticism but also active support which encourages creativity. Gardner (1993) was surprised to discover that each of the "creators" he studied relied on both emotional support and intellectual understanding during their most creative breakthroughs:

> First, the creator required both affective support from someone with whom he or she felt comfortable and cognitive support from someone who could understand the nature of the breakthrough. In some situations, the same person could supply both needs, while on other occasions, such double duty was unsuccessful or impossible. . . .
>
> As a psychologist interested in the *individual* creator, I was surprised by this discovery of the intensive social and affective forces that surround creative breakthroughs (p. 43).

While acknowledging the importance of emotional support to these "creators," Gardner (1993) observes that "a history of shyness and feelings of isolation as children appeared not infrequently" (p. 387). This sad truth—vital information for teachers and parents of creative children—is echoed by Mihaly Csikszentmihaly. In his study of creativity, he found this same pattern of loneliness in adolescence for people who later blossomed with creative genius (Csikszentmihaly,

1996, pp. 176–178). I have found this information comforting in understanding my own relative isolation during my teenage years, as well as that of my children. It allows me to understand my sons' loneliness and to approach their creativity with a sense of wonder and respect, instead of being alarmed that they are not participating in the "normal" devotion to the peer group considered essential to adolescence in America.

Pandora's Box: When Creativity Exposes Suffering or Danger

When a teacher creates an atmosphere for adolescents that flows with the "milk of human kindness," creative expression can become a vehicle for students to reveal their most joyful delights and their deepest sorrow and fear. "Every single year, I have a student who writes about abuse or suicide in their poetry. I've never taught poetry without something coming out," said Colleen Conrad (interview, 1999). "Kids who are being abused—it almost always comes out in their poetry."

Throughout the gateways explored in this book—connection, silence, meaning, and joy—we have heard students share painful stories that challenge us as teachers. One of the reasons we may be reluctant to create the conditions that invite soul into the classroom is what I call the "can of worms" or Pandora's Box argument. "We're not trained as therapists or counselors," many teachers say to me. "What if by inviting our students to share their feelings, we open a can of worms we just don't know how to handle?" This is a legitimate concern.

Working with a population of students who have suffered much, Conrad (interview, 1999) has learned how to respond to troubling information as she welcomes creativity into her classroom. Her experience can guide us when students' creative expression opens the door to their trauma or despair.

> I picked up a journal from a girl, which started by describing a rape she had experienced. It was like I was thrown into the pit of hell—it was gutwrenching. Page after page of experiences in vivid imagery. It made me physically ill.
>
> I had to put it away for a while and build up my resources. Then, knowing what I was going to face, I went back again.
>
> Then I talked to the girl. "If what you've written is something you've actually experienced," I said, "I want you to feel I'm a safe person to talk with because no child or woman should have to experience these things."

At first she said, "I can't talk about any of this."

I told her I would need to report the abuse. She had to under-stand that I must do this. But I would not share any of her private material, I assured her. "Suspected abuse" is all I have to report. And then, if she wanted to talk, she could come to me. And I filed the report.

A few weeks later I found on my desk a notebook full of her po-etry. I read the notebook and asked her to come after school and talk with me. She did start opening up after that. After she talked with me for a while, I asked her permission to put her in contact with a counselor. She agreed, and I worked together with a fe-male counselor at our school to arrange for her to talk with a counselor outside of school.

The first thing she was concerned about was that no one else would read her poetry. She seemed almost relieved that someone would take care of the abuse for her—she didn't know the re-sources available. She wasn't angry at all. She was hesitant to open up at first—she kept asking if someone else would see her poetry. Once she trusted that I wouldn't share her writing, she seemed relieved to talk.

Finding her way with common sense and caring through this first experience, Conrad discovered the principles that many teachers have found essential to safely navigate the dangerous feelings and facts that can emerge through creative expression—or even a simple "sharing cir-cle"—when a student feels either profoundly safe or desperate:

• We communicate up front to our students the limits to our confi-dentiality, which require us to report abuse or danger of suicide.

• While we make the report, we make every effort to collaborate with that student to find the most respectful way to alert authorities and seek outside help for that particular student.

• Avoiding the "Lone Ranger trap" that is so seductive with adoles-cents, we look for ways—as quickly as possible—to engage the support of a colleague at the school who is professionally trained to work with trauma and make referrals.

"The teacher's job is to listen, be nonjudgmental, acknowledge that this is a really big problem, and have the pragmatic conversation: 'Who do we need to talk to next?'" says Lisa Lopez Levers, chair of the counseling and human development program at the University of Rochester's School of Education.

"We tell teachers, 'When you get a sick feeling in your stomach, refer,'" says Sherry Dunn, principal of South Middle School in Arlington Heights, Illinois (cited in McGrath, 1998, p. 57).

As educators, we may have many good reasons to feel it is not our responsibility to deal with this "can of worms." But can we suppress the truth of our students' lives without suppressing their creative voice? And in the schoolyard killings of recent years, we see the price of ignoring the signals, excluding from the classroom the emotional and social confusion or anguish of students who had no adults to notice until it was too late. I am not suggesting that self-expression will come *only* through creative expression. Speaking from the heart may open Pandora's Box for students in any of the seven gateways; trauma may even surface through simple silence and stillness. Teachers who throw open the door to creative expression in the classroom must certainly be prepared to wrestle with this issue.

Other Obstacles

In encouraging the creativity of our students, it is not only the revelation of their pain or threats that challenges us to deal with difficult emotions. Adolescents may be beset with such anxiety about embarassing themselves that encouraging spontaneous creativity through dance or improvisation may backfire.

Movement teacher Joy Guarino (interview, 1999) finds that by 9th grade, or even younger for girls, students freeze up to avoid embarassment:

> They won't move except to walk around—9th and 10th grade are the toughest. They just stare. Then juniors and seniors begin to sense their own direction, and it really doesn't matter what people think of them; they start to open back up again.

Guarino also discovered that these same middle and early high school students can delight in the structured dance involved in school or class musicals. Chip Wood, in the last chapter, similarly described the value of highly structured country dancing for this age group. And although free-form improvisation may be difficult for most adolescents, providing structured role plays to explore problem solving offers the opportunity for both safety and creative risk.

Inherent in even the most healthy and exciting creative processes are moments of frustration and anxiety when our students become stuck. Why would we need the incubation phase at all if we could simply hammer out a solution with our will and our current skill level?

The waiting may seem interminable. It may seem like failure. Our culture gives little credence to the fertile possibilities of waiting. "I have seen it most often happen when a child gets really stuck when you ask them to write a poem," says Mary Lou Faddick in a 1999 interview. "These kids who are logical sequential thinkers do really well in math, but they get really annoyed when you present something too fuzzy to them."

How do we respond to the impatience and frustration that may seem unbearable to our students in the moments or days before illumination breaks through? Faddick describes her approach: "I ask them to just take this one word or idea and let it be still inside them for a while—overnight or 10 minutes in the classroom. Most of the time, kids will come up with something they feel good about—something that will lead them to a different place."

Perhaps the most important gift we can offer our students is to share our own delight in creative expression and model our own capacity for accepting the trials of the creative process. We can develop our own tolerance for not knowing, frustration, and the apparent detours and delays that lead to a genuinely innovative solution.

The Transforming Power of Creativity

> The spiritual life of the classroom is inextricably bound up with the notion of redemption, a word that means "buying back." Redemption is deliverance, a liberation from the obligation to suffer in the extreme. . . . Think of teaching as reclaiming students from anonymity and leading them toward deliverance. Interestingly enough, the student, thus redeemed and motivated, provides the teacher with a reciprocal liberation.
>
> —Principal Donald Wesley (1998/1999, p. 43)

When students find an opportunity to express their pain and challenges through creative expression, they often undergo healing transformations. Joy Guarino (interview, 1999) describes a series of classes with a group of children with Down syndrome, 12–18 years old:

> First we had a class where they just talked about how they feel about themselves. Then I gave them some movement options—low, middle, and high movement; back, forward, sideways, and then tempo changes—fast and slow; and then dynamic changes—closed and open. We played around with different kinds of movement.

"Some of you mentioned you get laughed at or people don't understand you. Show me how that feels." One little boy just sat on the floor and faced the wall. Then the entire group showed me how they felt about being laughed at. All their movements were closed, low, slow, and hidden.

After that, I encouraged them to talk about what it feels like to be accepted. They just wouldn't talk. So I called out positive feelings and asked them to show the movement that expressed that feeling. Slowly they began to tell me about good things that were happening in their lives—times of feeling loved or truly feeling a part of a team. The movement then became more open, and high and much faster.

"Show me a shape of which one you would rather feel," I asked them, and they all made high and open movements. "I want you to try to carry that with you so when someone is laughing at you, you can make that shape of knowing you do appreciate yourself."

Eventually they came from moving all alone to moving with each other and all dancing and laughing together.

Parker Palmer once spoke of the soul as "like a wild animal . . . exceedingly shy" and reluctant to reveal itself. He talked of how respectful and tender we must be to draw it out of hiding. "If we go crashing through the woods, screaming and yelling for the soul to come out, it will evade us all day and night" (cited in Glazer, 1999, p. 16). Creative expression—the opportunity to move laterally through symbol and metaphor, representing thoughts, feelings, and experiences in a nonlinear way—can be one of our most important allies in inviting the soul of young people into the classroom.

Though encouraging creativity is not new to the mission of schooling, it is imperiled today. Too often, we see it as a luxury and a distraction to the real work of the core curriculum. Or we want to avoid the unsettling feelings that may emerge from creative expression.

But creativity in the classroom is vital to both the survival of soul and the success of learning. "Creativity nourishes the soul," says Laura Simms in her 1999 interview, "because it is the language of the soul." When creativity breaks through, both teacher and student come alive. We connect deeply to ourselves and others, imbue life with freshness and meaning, and experience the delight that comes with transcending old or limited ways of thinking and doing. Mind, body, heart, and spirit come together to spark the passion that fuels the motivation to learn, to contribute, and to savor our infinite capacity for growth.

7 *Transcendence*

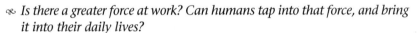

 ⚭ *Is there a greater force at work? Can humans tap into that force, and bring it into their daily lives?*

 ⚭ *Do our minds have barriers to understanding certain things, like everlasting and always? Or are there ways to open up parts of the brain and tap into different vibrations?*

 ⚭ *What can I do to really feel peaceful most of the time?*

 ⚭ *Will I be able to pass these limits that I feel on my mind?*

 ⚭ *It amazes me how much more you can do than you think you can.*

 ⚭ *Is there magic?*

 ⚭ *Why does death often seem much more inviting than life?*

For many years, I was reluctant to talk to parents or educators about the urge for transcendence. Because this need is specifically about reaching beyond ordinary life and consciousness, it seemed more closely linked to religion than to school. But two experiences compelled me to begin finding the words—and courage—to broach the subject of transcendence: drugs and suicide.

One year, some parents in a school I knew well reported to me on the epidemic use of LSD among a large portion of the junior class. I was just as alarmed as the parents were. At first, the students' use of LSD made no sense to me. Many teenagers find the "high" from alcohol or marijuana "fun" in the short run; doubt or denial prevents them from seeing the dangerous long-term consequences. But LSD does not produce an easy-going "high"; it often triggers a loss of ego boundaries and hallucinations that are often troubling and can be terrifying. Why would large numbers of students voluntarily subject themselves to this ordeal?

After exploring this question with some of my students, I concluded that the use of LSD and other hallucinogens was the desperate attempt of some usually thoughtful students to explore nonordinary states of consciousness. *"The true feeling for nature for me comes from marijuana and other drugs that in fact release the images that I have to hold, which is the epitome of myself,"* writes one student anonymously. *"Mushrooms made me see this side only because I let out my true emotions and feelings of being free with nature as one."* Living in a culture in which none of their parents or teachers were willing to talk with them about the human yearning for transcendence, they sought their own (self-destructive) paths.

Another student, also writing anonymously, wrestles with this curiosity: *"I guess I've been thinking of different ways people interpret reality and relate to each other. I've also been thinking about how ingesting certain chemicals can make someone interpret reality in a different way."*

"Adolescents of all ages need ecstatic experience to become adult," writes Neville (1989, p. 248), "and if the culture does not provide it they will seek it in any case, often in ways which do them harm." Like other adults, I had been unwilling to talk to the young about this dimension of human experience common to most cultures throughout time.

"Unfortunately, we achieve ecstasy these days in the worst of ways," writes Willard Johnson, "as by-products of accidents and near-death experiences, through hallucinogenic 'trips,' through borderline cult experiences directed at times by near psychopathic personalities, or through such uncontrollable media as alcohol and drug abuse . . . to name a few of the many ways by which this deepest of human experiences can sometimes be produced" (cited in Neville, 1989, p. 248). These self-destructive distortions of the urge for transcendence fueled my determination to understand this gateway to the soul in education.

The second phenomenon that spurred my investigations was teenage suicide. Several years ago, I read a *New York Times* article about the double suicide of healthy, successful, affluent Long Island teenagers. The community was shocked and bewildered. "Why?" asked the principal, with tears in his eyes. "These were not high-risk kids." They were not the children of dispossessed and broken families and neighborhoods, not the children of abusive or negligent parents, not dropouts.

I felt the same shock when I listened to both adults and teenagers who were plagued by images of suicide. I heard a confusion in their thinking: They seemed to be mistaking a hunger for transcendence with a longing for death. Lacking any understanding of how to find serenity, beauty, and mystery in healthy ways, they had fallen in love with death, romanticizing death as poets have done through the centuries as a direct route to mystical union. Although such confusion does not account for the teenagers who attempt suicide out of the many sources of hopelessness and despair, it was a clue that some suicidal impulses could be redirected into a quest for life-affirming experiences of transcendence.

"'Ecstasy' is not a word we use very often in writing about education. Neither is 'joy,' for that matter," writes Neville (1989). "Even if we can dismiss the religious associations of ecstasy, our conventional fantasies of education do not easily accommodate the idea of teaching children to transcend their ordinary mental states" (p. 247).

Despite my fear that the community would misunderstand my efforts, I resolved to discuss this matter with parents, teachers, and students. I wanted to find a better understanding of the basic human need for transcendence and appropriate ways to address it in school.

What Is Transcendence?

For many years, I understood transcendence only in terms of mystical experiences. Then I discovered a broader view. I saw that when students are "lost" or "immersed" in play, dance, or any other form of the creative process, they often experience a kind of transcendence described as "flow" by research psychologist Mihaly Csikszentmihaly (1996), who popularized this concept in his study of experiences that can provide "flashes of intensity" against the "dull background" of ordinary days.

> A person in flow is completely focused. There is no space in consciousness for distracting thoughts, irrelevant feelings. . . . Self-consciousness disappears, yet one feels stronger than usual. The sense of time is distorted; hours seem to pass by in minutes. When a person's entire being is stretched in the full functioning of body and mind, whatever one does become worth doing for its own sake (p. 71).

I also discovered in Weaver and Cotrell's (1992) schema of "spiritual urges" a definition that went well beyond the mystical aspect of transcendence and allowed me to see how educators can nurture this need in students: "To transcend is to rise above or pass beyond a human limit," they write. "It involves moving beyond everyday dimensions of life and its usual limitations" (p. 433).

In providing opportunities for students to reach for excellence and extraordinary achievement in academics, athletics, and artistic performance, teachers support this spiritual yearning of adolescents and young adults to "rise above a human limit." I'm not suggesting that a teacher or coach demand perfection. My students often refer to a distinction I share from Angeles Arrien (1993) about the difference between perfection and excellence:

> Perfection does not tolerate mistakes, whereas excellence incorporates and learns from mistakes (p. 67).

In guiding our students toward transcendence, we draw forth *their* yearnings rather than impose *our* own expectations; we recognize and support students' own passions to take an extraordinary leap beyond what has been their usual performance.

This chapter explores six domains in which young people may experience a transcendent moment:

- Athletic, academic, and artistic performance.
- Adventure learning.
- Transcending prejudice and stereotypes.
- Transcendence through suffering.
- Sharing mysterious experiences.
- Nonordinary states of consciousness.

Athletic, Academic, and Artistic Performance

"It looks comfortable," says Sarah, picking up the old running shoe that someone has brought as a symbol of what is important to that person. "Soft and worn-in, that's what drew me to it. I bet I know who it belongs to," she says, looking at the track star in the class.

"You're right," says Drew, "it's mine. This is hard to talk about because I have to say that running is almost a 'spiritual' experience for me."

He pauses, letting the word *spiritual* settle out of its awkward place in his mouth and in this room. He holds the shoe upright before us. "What I mean is that these soft leather uppers represent the ease, the calm I need to create in myself in order to begin a race."

Drew turns the shoe over to reveal long metal spikes sticking out below. "But these ferocious-looking spikes represent the power and ruthlessness that come through me, from I don't know where, that allow me to actually win the race."

Athletics is a natural place in school for transcendence. The Greek word for the hero's labors, *athlos*, reminds us that the ancient Greeks saw athletics not simply as sports but as heroics. "The quest of the athlete is endowed with a sacred attribute, marked by his *agon,* that is, his struggle to overcome the limitations of his nature" (Kamperidis, 1992, p. 14).

Even during practice, a student may discover the altered biochemical state of "runner's high": Endorphins flood the body with a feeling of extraordinary well being and grace. In any sport, the intense state of focus and repetitive movements can lead some students into a state of extraordinary clarity, serenity, and a more balanced perspective.

In addition, consider the state of calm Drew creates *before* the run. Most students are left on their own to discover how to do this; and many never do. When athletic (or drama or vocal) coaches give students the awareness and tools to find that calm and focus, they help them both overcome, or "transcend," the usual performance "nerves" and discover that extraordinary power that allows the student to excel.

Another student described a tennis match where she was exhausted after winning the first set. Despite the high stakes and all the people watching, she simply could not muster the energy and lost the second set. "We sort of gave up at that point," her friends and family reported to her later. "You looked so dehydrated, so beat, we wished you didn't even have to play that third set."

But in the second game of the third set, with her opponent now cocky, Alisha felt something come through her that she had never experienced before:

> It was an energy—or maybe will or determination—or all of it. It was so powerful, and I didn't know where it was coming from. But I seized it. I became it. I pushed through all that heavy fatigue, and I won the match. And what was really righteous was that my parents saw it, too. They saw the change come over me, and they could talk with me about it. That made it even more special.

Some students can experience this same power in academic striving. When he visited after his first year of college, Zack told me about taking a course in his intended major—a course usually taken only by upperclassmen. The professor noted that Zack's proposal for the final paper looked more like a senior thesis than an ordinary paper. Instead of discouraging Zack from his vision, or clamping down judgmentally for violating the terms of the assignment, this teacher encouraged him and offered to evaluate it as a senior thesis. Fellow students discouraged him, noting that this professor was excruciatingly tough on even upperclassmen. But Zack enthusiastically pursued his innovative approach. As a freshman, he completed his senior thesis and was awarded an outstanding grade.

During an inservice training, one teacher shared an experience from his own childhood that went the other way:

> I had been having trouble with math in 4th grade. One time, I finally got a 100 on a math test. This was such an achievement! But Mrs. Pinkus took the moment away from me. "So finally you did decently on something in here," she said; and I felt humiliated again. Like there was nothing I could ever do to really succeed.

How we respond to our students' striving can determine whether we undercut self-worth or encourage a transcendent moment.

So, for many students, experiences like this are not just about winning or doing well. When students experience a power that takes them to new levels in sports, academics, music, or performance of any kind, we help consolidate the spiritual meaning by giving them opportunities to talk about it and be honored by others who recognize the larger importance of the experience.

In performance, transcendence often comes when we strive to go beyond routine effort, beyond perceived limits. In encouraging such striving among our students, we can call forth a rigorous discipline even when it appears unwelcome. This growth-promoting experience is totally unlike the dangerous highs that come from abdicating will and critical thinking to a drug or charismatic cult leader. Healthy experiences of transcendence require not only will but a conscious decision to be open to mystery, such as the mysterious power that both Drew and Alisha discovered.

Adventure Learning

As in athletics, the physicalness of adventure-based learning can provide a doorway for many students into transcendence. Techniques from this field are used broadly in many schools—in student orientation programs at the beginning of the school year, social and emotional learning programs, after-school programs, and expeditionary-learning charter schools. These methods, such as ropes courses, rock-climbing, river rafting, "solos," and team-building challenges, encourage students to overcome their fears and perceived limits. Many students report "peak experiences" that inspire hope and self-confidence. New educational research shows lasting benefits to students from this form of learning (see Viadero, 1997).

Listening to students describe these experiences, I often sense the presence of the spiritual dimension. Some adventure staff are specifically trained to acknowledge this dimension, to name or deepen the spiritual development afforded by these programs. Many are unaware of the potential spiritual effect of these activities and lose an opportunity to nourish the growth of students. In some cases, they can harm students by not preparing them adequately for "reentry" into ordinary life from such a peak experience (see Chapter 8).

Transcending Prejudice and Stereotypes

∞ *Will I ever be able to go somewhere where I won't be prejudged and people's opinions of me will be based on my actions and not by what I look like or where I'm from?*

∞ *How do you change injustice? Why do people hurt each other because of a belief or opinion?*

∞ *Why are people at this school so judgmental of others, and protective of their "social status"—we're all the same—we all want to be accepted, but those "accepted few" aren't very accepting of others! Ironique, eh?*

∞ *Why do people judge someone before they know them?*

∞ *Are men and women truly different?*

Every school has its cliques, its scapegoats, and the dividing line of gender. Most U.S. schools also live with differences in class, race, and culture. In my teaching experience, one of the most powerful experiences with transcendence I observe is when students transform rigid and hostile boundaries between groups and individuals into mutual respect, unity, and even affection.

In a senior class in Colorado, I watched two young men—a burly football player and a tall, slender drama student—scale the walls of prejudice and discover what it feels like to overcome entrenched divisiveness.

Kyle was the most flamboyant student I have known. He chose each outfit with a sense of theatricality and style that in the '40s might have been called "dapper." His clothes were not feminine, but his attention to fashion and his devotion to theater disturbed some of the more macho students. In our class, he graced us with an unusual combination of cheerful good nature and courageous honesty and thoughtfulness.

Halfway through the semester, Kyle came in early to talk with staff before the other students came in. He was upset, and we encouraged him to talk about it in our "council" meeting. When the "talking stone" came to him, Kyle began:

> I know we have another topic, but I have to talk about something that happened in the lunchroom this week. I was with some of my friends from theater and vocal. We just kind of came together spontaneously and started to sing. Other kids started to gather around us and encouraged us to go for it; you know, to sing louder and really get into it. So we did. We were really jamming, and it felt great.
>
> Then this group of jocks gathered in their own little circle and started jeering us. Next thing they were throwing spitballs. Spit. God, it was painful. So humiliating. So unnecessary. And I have to say . . .

Kyle turned now and looked across the circle at Mike, cocaptain of the football team. "I have to say, Mike, that I saw you among them—and that really, really hurt."

Mike looked down at his shoes. His face was red. Kyle passed the stone, and it was close to 10 minutes before it got to Mike. He didn't respond; he chose to address the theme of the council, speaking briefly and without much feeling. Kyle was upset after class; we honored him for speaking his truth and encouraged him to be patient.

Weeks later, at the end of the senior retreat, Mike spoke up in a group session. He looked at Kyle.

> I had these prejudices when I came into the group. But my heart has been opened to you, Kyle. I feel a lot of love for you now. I really value you, and I just wish I had more time to get to know you.

In the flurry of hugs after the closing council, Mike walked over to Kyle, wrapping his husky arms in a warm embrace around Kyle's delicate frame.

When students find themselves overcoming deep and persistent divisions in their own relationships and in the life of the community, the entire class shares a moment of transcendence. Prejudice and ideological conflicts can be transcended in classrooms where authentic community is achieved. So can scapegoating:

"You guys, a lot of you, were the same people that used to throw food at me in 7th grade," said Richard, in tears on the last day of his Senior Passage Course.

> I was the geek, the dork you all made fun of. I'm still not cool. I know it. I still look different and have my peculiar ways. But you

guys have really taken me in; you've accepted me, you've respected me. I know how far you've come.

The experience of resolving deeply entrenched conflicts, of feeling
respect where once there was hate and mistrust, is a transforming event
in what Nel Noddings calls "everyday spirituality" (cited in Halford,
1998/1999, p. 31).

In my own work, the experiences of genuinely meeting somebody
across a divide of hatred, disrespect, or stereotyping have come primarily through *indirect* means. Through telling their stories, laughing and
playing together, students have discovered a new respect, openness,
and affection for one another. "This class has truly proven to me that
everyone contains such personal beauty, it amazes me and only makes
me want to get to know people better," writes one senior.

Other educators take a more *direct* approach. In *Waging Peace in Our
Schools,* Linda Lantieri and Janet Patti (1996) look closely at the concept of oppression and talk about groups of privilege and nonprivilege.
They discuss "isms"—ageism, sexism, adultism, racism—and how they
play themselves out in our communities, our schools, and our own
lives. The authors describe practices in their curriculum that allow educators to directly engage the divisive issues of bias and oppression in
ways that are specifically designed to close this painful breach.

Both indirect and direct approaches can lead to transcendent moments when *compassion, respect, and understanding replace prejudice, hatred, and fear.* Each teacher and each school community need to decide
how to integrate these approaches into their curriculum and school
life.

Transcending Gender Polarization

෨ *Why is the way guys think so different from girls?*

෨ *Can men really care about women?*

෨ *Why do people of the opposite sex really intrigue me and yet deep down
scare me when I know they shouldn't?*

One of the most common and archetypal divides that produces
mistrust and misinterpretation is the gap between men and women.
Young people are enormously curious about the experience and per-
ceptions of the opposite sex. They yearn to transcend the misunder-
standing and miscommunication between men and women that have
led to so many broken families. Boys and girls in grades 7–9 welcome
structured, safe opportunities in school to ask respectful questions of
each other and answer what they choose to answer.

In the higher grades, the conversation goes far deeper; and the distrust may be far more challenging to overcome. One girl gained a new outlook after a dialogue about gender on her senior retreat:

> I finally realized that we put men in such a horrible position sometimes. When Pete said, "We don't know! We don't know how to treat you, how to love you women. It's a secret kept from us!" I was so touched by how earnest he was, by his genuine curiosity.
>
> I see now that men are also emotionally deep, and that by tapping into that wisdom—you can get the complete picture.

Creating opportunities for students to transcend the barriers of gender, class, race, and belief not only nourishes the spirit but is also a key to civil society. How can we allow students to graduate from high school without being challenged to see and transcend the prejudices and stereotypes we all grow up with? Hate crimes are consistently committed by those who had their biases reinforced rather than lifted during their early years.

Students who have had opportunities in school to overcome bias often state that they will never look in the same way at people who are different from them. "What has been such a pleasant surprise about this class," said Eli, "is that I have learned that each person has special qualities and gifts to give when you see who they are behind the surface."

As teachers, we are also profoundly affected by what our own culture and institutions have disowned and despised. We, too, have been touched by this "collective shadow" (Zweig & Abrams, 1991), which takes the form of scapegoating, prejudice, and discrimination. Even when teachers strive to treat all people with fairness and dignity, the corrosive residue of prejudice we have absorbed from our surroundings may affect our relationships with certain students, colleagues, and parents. Taking time together in a supportive environment, we can uncover unconscious negative attitudes about some students or discover what keeps us from setting appropriate boundaries with others.

Transcendence Through Suffering

❧ *How far can I be stretched, how much adversity can I stand?*
❧ *Will I be able to look at the positive and reconstruct my life when I hit a major depression?*
❧ *Why do you learn the greatest lessons from the hardest things?*

For many years, when I asked my seniors to tell a story about a time when their spirit was nourished, the stories I heard were what we would ordinarily call "positive" experiences. I certainly expected an upbeat tale from Connie, the stereotype of the "all-American" perfect beauty. She was a cheerleader, always cracking jokes and surrounded by peers who adored her. Judging by appearances, Connie was cute and fun but not likely to have depth. But listen to her voice: "What I think really nourished my spirit," Connie began, pensively moving her tongue to feel the new tongue ring against her teeth, "was getting through that awful year in 8th grade when my dad was accused." She stopped and looked around the circle, then began again:

> I guess I thought most of you would know, but I suppose maybe a lot of you don't. My dad's a teacher, has been all his life. That year, some kid accused him of sexual misconduct. It was all over the place. Everyone knew. My Dad was suspended while they investigated. And everywhere we went, we all just felt so humiliated, it seemed unbearable.
>
> Well, we're a big family. Six kids. And my mom, she helped us see how important it was to trust our dad, to never lose faith in him or in God. And we all pulled together. And he was cleared, of course, and got his job back. But it was the strength I felt inside me, and inside my family, that nourished my spirit. More than anything else.

I realized later that, for Connie, this was a transcendent experience. She and her family had gone far beyond what felt like unsurmountable limits of suffering to sustain their love and faith.

We can help our students understand the opportunity to transcend suffering by the way we respond to it in our students' stories and in literature, history, and other subjects. "We so often give children a literary experience, but avoid the real-life talk," says Chip Wood in a 1999 interview. "We read Anne Frank but often don't talk about the student in class who is being ostracized." When suffering prompts us to discover courage, faith, compassion, forgiveness, truth-telling, or love—in ourselves or others—it may take us to heights and depths that surpass our ordinary life, our everyday experiences.

This is a perspective that students, like Connie, can best arrive at on their own, after they have had ample support and compassion for what they are going through. Especially in inner-city schools where children have faced frequent violence and abuse, teachers and counselors may need to remind students that they do not deserve the suffering they have endured, that it is not their fault, and that it is natural to feel anguish or rage. "So often here we have nothing in our experience that can relate to some of the horrors these kids experience," lamented a caring teacher from an urban school. "Sometimes I feel like I have nothing to bring them."

But we do have our compassion to bring to students. So do the other students, who may also find—in their caring for a classmate, friend, or community service client—that they are transcending their ordinary preoccupation with themselves.

Optional Only: On the Razor's Edge

Until now, I have addressed opportunities in the curriculum for fostering or acknowledging transcendent experiences most families and teachers would accept. The next sections venture into territory that may feel inappropriate for some parents who come from either the highly secular or fundamentalist ends of the spectrum of belief. Before initiating any of the practices that follow, teachers must consult with parents to determine what does and does not feel respectful of family traditions. Ideally this involves dialogue, in person, during an evening meeting with parents. Teachers not only describe the practices and theories behind them, but give parents some concrete experiences with potentially controversial practices. Parents are encouraged to ask questions and to work with the teacher to refine these teaching strategies to ensure respect for family beliefs. Parents can then provide written permission for what feels comfortable to them and sign "opt-out" forms for what does not.

As teachers, then, we must wrestle with the dilemma of whether to proceed with a practice that troubles some families enough to opt out. Sharing this dilemma with a colleague or supervisor is essential to gaining some perspective on our own positions. In my own experience, if I cannot find the language and common understanding to ease the concerns of families, I prefer to include all the students and omit certain practices. We can also find ways—such as the "witness" role—to offer the practice to some students without making others feel excluded.

With this caveat in mind, let's explore some of the more controversial aspects of transcendence that may be offered in school.

Sharing the Mystery

❧ *I feel like I can see what people are feeling.*

❧ Deja vu—*why does everything seem like it's happened before?*

❧ *Will we (humans) be psychic in my lifetime?*

Many students have had experiences that feel mysterious or paranormal. In a reason-based culture and educational system, students are shy and afraid to talk about such transcendent moments. We can support them by giving them opportunities to speak to a group of respectful peers and teachers about "nonordinary" experiences they have had inside or outside of their school life.

In a 10th grade "check-in" circle, Lana shared that she had almost been hit by a car the previous day:

> I was about to step off this curb, and for some reason—I mean for no reason, really—I just stopped. A car swerved around the corner into the very spot I was going to walk across. Isn't that weird? I mean, I don't know why I stopped. All I know is that it saved my life.

The group asked if we could have a council on "weird" times like that. Students talked about times they knew, felt, or saw something for which there was no easy explanation. This council helped all of us appreciate this mysterious dimension of our lives.

In his research for *The Secret Life of Kids,* James Peterson (1987) encouraged and gave voice to many children who told him stories of extraordinary experiences. Robert Coles (1990) also gave a respectful audience to children he describes in "Visionary Moments" in *The Spiritual Life of Children*. At first, Coles could not really attend to some of the children who had experienced visions. His psychoanalytic training inclined him to reduce to pathology any accounts that did not fit rational explanation. A Native American girl who shared her visions with him stirred confusion in his scientific mind:

> I asked her whether she was awake or asleep when she saw her ancestors. I knew she was not psychotic, and having worked for years with Hopis, I understood their vivid metaphoric language (p. 152).

Coles struggled with his bias, but was plagued by derisive terms for what he was hearing. "'Magical thinking,' a phrase that I learned to use a lot during my residency in child psychiatry, descended on my mind rather often when Natalie talked," writes Coles. Growing increasingly aware that these terms and definitions were "psychological or cultural standards," he gave these children the open-minded hearing that makes him such an extraordinary explorer into the riches of children's inner lives (Coles, 1990, pp. 153–158).

Coles wrestled with the personal and professional judgments that were barriers to listening to these children with honor. His integrity is an inspiration to us as teachers to examine our own prejudgments and intentions if we are going to invite students to speak about matters of the soul. Educator Chip Wood (interview, 1999) shares a warning about what happens when we don't:

> I was observing a middle school teacher. He had asked kids to think about their secret places that were special to them. He asked them to consciously go to that place and think about what it meant to them and why it was such a special place. Then they wrote about it and shared their writing in small conferences with peers to clarify and polish their essays.
>
> I was there the day he asked them to share their writing out loud with the class. A girl volunteered to go first; she shared a hauntingly beautiful story of a tree by a stream in a back pasture, behind the trailer where she lived. It was a place no one knew about and where she could have her own space, her own thoughts. A place where she came to deep and important understandings of the world.
>
> The room was hushed with feeling, and into the silence came the teacher's abrupt command. "NEXT!" he said in a voice devoid of feeling, turning the entire exercise into a mechanical task.
>
> I felt that she had put her whole soul out there. And there was no response. No affirmation or appreciation of what she had offered. The other kids immediately reined in their stories because what had seemed like a sacred space was ignored, destroyed, unrecognized by this teacher.
>
> It made me realize that toying with spirituality, if you don't know what you're doing, can be more damaging than just ignoring it. And I realized that when you evoke the children's souls, which are much more on the surface, you can be suddenly surprised by the appearance of your own soul in the same space. Some teachers may be quite unprepared for that.

When the lesson plan is more important than the student's feelings or experience, when we are preoccupied with "doing it right" and "covering the material," we often forget to open our hearts to our students.

When we create a safe, respectful space for young people to tell their stories of mysterious experiences to a community of their own peers and teachers, even just speaking out about the experiences is nourishing to the spirit. Here's an example from a Senior Passages Course.

Many weeks into the course, after the group had established genuine trust and respect for one another, we addressed the theme of spirit. Two girls in the class, each of whom had recently experienced a loss in the immediate family, took the opportunity to speak about death. Nell, whose brother had been killed in an automobile accident the previous spring, began:

> After my brother's funeral, we went back to my grandparents' hotel room. I couldn't stand being inside with everyone—I felt claustrophobic and needed some fresh air. Their room had a balcony, so I walked out by myself. When I looked down at the ground, I saw my shadow. I looked behind me to see where the sun was coming from and then looked down again. This time I saw two shadows, one beside the other. I looked to either side of me, and no one was there. Then I knew.

> I knew my brother was with me at that moment and that he would always be with me when I needed him.

Told with almost childlike simplicity, Nell's story stirred a sense of wonder and awe throughout the room. Tanya's story took a different turn:

> It was the night before my father left to go hiking for the day. I was going out that night after dinner, kind of rushing around getting ready before we ate. My dad was sitting on the couch in the family room, right next to the kitchen where my mom was cooking. As I walked by, he pulled me playfully down on his lap. "Did I ever tell you that you are the best daughter a father could ever hope to have?"

> I smiled at him. "Yes, Daddy, you have."

> "Well, I thought I'd tell you again, because I am just so proud of you. . . ." and he went on and on about who I was now that I was practically all grown up.

> Then he yelled to my mom in the kitchen, "You are the most beautiful woman in the world!" He turned back to me and told me that my mom was the dearest, finest wife a man could ever want and how after 20 years together, he loved her more and more each day. Mom popped her head out of the kitchen, and the three of us tumbled together on the couch in a hug like we hadn't had since I was little.

> And then we had dinner, and I went out. I never saw him that night when I came home, or in the morning, because he left early for his hike. It was a freak accident that killed him—we

> were all in shock for weeks. When I finally remembered our last night, I kept wondering—did he know something? Of course he couldn't know. But he couldn't have said a better good-bye to us if it had all been planned.

When a loved one dies, students begin to wonder about or actually experience the possibilities of transcending ordinary reality. Other students connect their experience of the mysterious directly to God:

> When my stepdad had surgery—teetering between recovery and not—I was worried about him. I left the hospital, and there was a huge rainbow. I've always loved rainbows, and I thought now about the one God delivered to earth after the Flood—the peace after the storm. I remembered God's promise that he would never do that again. It felt like a sign. I felt my stepdad would get better. And he did."

In this chapter, I have shared examples of students being remarkably articulate about mysterious moments where they felt they had transcended ordinary ways of being in the world. These experiences, however, often elude words. Using art and music—giving students the opportunity to express their memories and yearning for mystery through images and symbols—can also nourish this aspect of their development.

"Altered States"

- ❧ *Will I evolve to higher states of consciousness?*
- ❧ *How do I rise above the banality of life as I live it and remain in a transcendental state?*
- ❧ *Is it possible to get in touch with the feelings and experiences the Greeks spoke of when they performed the Eleusinian Mysteries?*

This chapter would not be complete without a consideration of nonordinary or mystical states of consciousness. What can we learn from brain research, mind-body health practices, and various methods of "superlearning"? Some researchers emphasize enhancements to learning and health that can come from helping students learn to control and shift their brain waves and quality of attention (Ostrander & Schroeder, 1979, pp. 63–76). When we consider the use of "altered states" in education, we need to be aware of both the dangers and opportunities of some of the most common practices.

Benefits to Students. I have found that *relaxation exercises,* which include attending to breath and muscle relaxation, can help students become alert and focused, as well as foster a more harmonious learning environment. I have also worked with *visualization* or *guided imagery* and see the benefits, for many children, of awakening the imagination, satisfying curiosity about "altered states of consciousness" in healthy ways, and gaining new insight about their goals and gifts.

When Good Intentions Go Too Far. When teachers talk with students about "inner guides" or "receiving guidance from within," parents from certain faiths fear their children are being led to blasphemy. From their metaphysical perspective, guidance comes only from God, as written in the Bible and interpreted by the minister. This metaphysical dispute goes all the way back in U.S. history to the Massachusetts Bay Colony when Anne Hutchinson was expelled for encouraging others to gather together for contemplation in search of the "indwelling spirit." Many educators are shocked when parents object to guided imagery and are angry when they hear about lawsuits against using such "New Age" practices in the classroom. When we understand how the very premises of this method may violate the faith of certain families, we can find mutually respectful solutions.

In addition, I share the concerns of parents who are wary of what teachers might "input" into their children's minds after using relaxation exercises, which could move some students into a highly receptive state. We teachers already have enormous influence because of the power of our position of authority. We must be extremely cautious and thoughtful about how we speak to students when they are deeply relaxed.

Heather Koerner (interview, 1999), associate editor of *Teachers in Focus,* a journal of Focus on the Family, emphasizes the risks of visualization:

> To me it's going too far—the teacher taking that role as a spiritual guide in visualization. I am not comfortable with a teacher leading children in that way. Children, even in high school, are so impressionable about a teachers' leanings. Even with the most benevolent intentions, it is wrong.

Without proper training and self awareness, it is easy to manipulate or instill our own images, feelings and beliefs. Some of the early books on visualization for children, while excellent in many ways, include scripts with spiritual imagery that can rightly be called "New Age" and, used in public schools, would violate both the First Amendment and the beliefs of certain families. I am also concerned about teachers' using guided imagery or deep relaxation to evoke painful emotions or memories—a therapeutic method that is not meant for the classroom.

Proceeding with Care. With these cautions in mind, I believe that some forms of visualization can be beneficial to students at all grade levels when used appropriately. If teachers have determined that their particular classroom community is not metaphysically offended by this practice, and if they use visualization to *elicit, not instill,* images and thoughts from their students, they can greatly enhance learning, reduce stress, and strengthen the imagination and creativity of their students.

Elissa Weindling (interview, 1999), a teacher at University Heights High School in the Bronx, regularly uses a visualization in which she invites students to go in their imagination to a place that feels very safe and comfortable and to create whatever they want it to be. She encourages the students to explore that space with all their senses and then gives them up to 10 minutes of silence to be there. She states:

> My first year of teaching, they loved it so much that we made it a part of every class. Our kids are so tense, they look like they never really relax. But in their journals, many write it was the first time they had a chance to release their own stress and that they saw they could do something about their stress. One boy always envisions himself in the future, with his own family, in a car with a pet, traveling on a trip, feeling safe and loved.

Toward the end of the visualization, Weindling suggests that if there's anything they want to take back with them from that place that would make them feel good, they can do so with their imagination. "Frequently, kids will bring something back, or mention people who have died who were there with them in their safe place." As a closing, Weindling reminds them that they can always create this safe place and have control in their minds to make it what they want.

Most students, particularly those with mood and attention-deficit disorders, can be helped by brief guided excursions into an alpha brain-wave state because it helps the brain to reorganize and reintegrate (Adolph, personal communication, 1999). Used at intervals throughout the day, this triggering of an alpha state temporarily produces a shift into a more balanced biochemical and brain-wave pattern. The reduction of anxiety and calming of the nervous system can be invaluable for students seeking to control their emotions and impulses.

Of course, not all students will learn to shift their brain-wave pattern simply from silence, relaxation, or visualization in the classroom. But in my own experience with students—from kindergartners to seniors—most young people show a marked shift toward calm and clarity after such exercises. One of my students, a baseball player who surprised me by signing up for an elective minicourse in visualization I offered one year for seniors, reported that after doing the relaxation and visualization every day for a week, he had slept through the night for the first time in high school.

Meditation: A Word of Caution

What about teaching meditation to our students? First, meditation, even described by names like "the relaxation response," may violate the beliefs of some families. In this case, as in relaxation exercises, visualization, and guided imagery, we must hold dialogues with parents to clarify and refine our practices.

If the parent community is supportive, however, meditation can lead to an altered state of consciousness that satisfies students' hunger for transcendence. There are documented benefits to learning and health, as Neville (1989) states:

> When children learn to meditate, they show less overt anxiety, more tolerance for frustration, less restlessness, greater ability to attend to a task. They have fewer headaches; their sleep improves. If the source of their anxiety is specific they become able to talk about it without distress. In short, they are happier (p. 245).

Nevertheless, we have to think carefully about teaching children to "meditate." I prefer to offer them time for *quiet reflection;* and if they choose to meditate, encourage only brief excursions into this realm.

Perhaps the reason that many adolescents are reluctant to meditate is that intuitively they know that moving into a prolonged egoless state can be dangerous, whether it is induced by drugs, sexual surrender, or even meditation. As James Peterson (1987) states:

> The psychological task of children . . . is to develop a masterful ego. . . . Such an ego will be able to cope effectively with life, and to become a responsible person in society. As psychologists such as Erik Erikson point out, this consolidation of ego identity is not nearly completed until late adolescence (p. 209).

While for adults, spiritual growth may mean surrendering the ego, children and youth who let go of their still-fragile egos may not be able to get them back. This can be frightening. "Meditation practices aimed at ego dissolution actually work against the direction of child development" (Peterson, 1987, p. 210).

In addition, the still-forming ego of the child or adolescent is not strong enough to contain and safely process the powerful energies that may be released through prolonged meditative practice. Peterson (1987) continues: "The basic problem with teaching children spiritual practices . . . is that these meditations, breath exercises, yogas, and mantras actually *work,* releasing energies that children literally are not equipped to handle" (p. 210).

I am also urging caution here because I am concerned that some teachers and parents who are drawn to a book called *The Soul of Education* may tend to overdo it with children. Some of these adults may be in the delightful "discovery" phase of their own spiritual journey. Eager to share what works for them with the children they love, they may obtain dangerous results. We must evaluate such practices in light of what we know about children's growth.

When considering transcendence as a gateway to the soul in education, we must remember that to nourish spiritual development does *not* mean that we take on the role of "spiritual guide." As Peterson (1987) reminds us, "Just because a philosophy or spiritual practice is good and right for an adult, that is no indication that it will be good and right for a child" (p. 220). Though you may be inspired by methods for achieving transcendence in your own life, that doesn't mean those methods belong in the classroom.

Whether or not they know the word *transcendence,* young people are curious about unexplained, mind-altering, or mysterious experiences. They may have had a spiritual or triumphant moment as a child when they felt they had entered another realm, a place of exquisite aliveness that they long to return to. Or as adolescents, they may be yearning for "more," when the quick pleasure of popular culture no longer satisfies an emptiness inside. As educators, we are often afraid to talk with parents and students about this ambiguous, controversial dimension of human experience. We cannot, however, afford to avoid it. If we do not guide young people into this domain, *they will go there without us*—and many will lose their way.

We must search together with our colleagues and the parents in our community for a language and for common principles that will guide us to be safe and respectful as we teach the children about this ancient human yearning. The key to nourishing transcendence in school is not to impose *our* views but to listen to *theirs.*

8 *Initiation*

- ❧ *Why am I so anxious to leave, but I'm afraid to start anew?*
- ❧ *Why can't we just play more and be happy like we used to?*
- ❧ *Will my parents be supportive once I'm in college?*
- ❧ *Will I get burnt out of school and too stressed out next year?*
- ❧ *Why do my parents seem like they refuse to acknowledge my growth? I feel like they should treat me as an equal, but they still play silly parent/child power games like I am 14 years old.*
- ❧ *Will I survive in the "real world" when no one is around to take care of me?*

Traditional cultures taught us that adolescence is a particularly important point in the spiritual life cycle. Virtually every preindustrial culture provided rites of initiation that helped their young navigate the dangerous waters between childhood and adulthood. When the adolescents' yearning for initiation is not met by responsible elders, young people often devise ritual actions that can turn destructive and alienating. Without constructive rites of passage provided by adults, teenagers in our communities have created their own badges of adulthood—from the relatively benign driver's licenses, proms, and graduation ceremonies, to the more dangerous extremes of binge drinking, first baby, first jail sentence, or first murder. "If the fires that innately burn inside youths are not intentionally and lovingly added to the hearth of community,"says poet Michael Meade (1993, p. 19), "they will burn down the structures of culture, just to feel the warmth."

The Need for Initiation

The term *rites of passage* often evokes images of tribal villages where boys are snatched away from their parents to be tried and tested by life-threatening ordeals that will make them men. Or day-long celebrations of the whole community for a girl's first menses. And although indigenous peoples have indeed created rituals to initiate their young, this cry for initiation from the adolescent soul surfaces with striking universality.

In the United States, we have undergone rapid technological change; an ongoing influx of new cultures; and a dissolution of traditional values, communities, and institutions that once bound us together. Our adolescents have also lost their moorings. "The collapse of traditional cultures," writes Meade (1993, p. 19), "the loss of shared myths and rituals that enfold the individual into the group, and the spread of modern industrial societies are producing generations of unbonded children and adults who are not initiated to the purpose and meaning of their own lives."

Although some American teenagers are blessed with meaningful confirmations, *Bar* and *Bat Mitzvahs, Quinceañera* ceremonies in the Mexican community, or initiation journeys offered by the Buddhist or Native American or African American communities, most of our youth today have no opportunity to be guided through the loneliness and confusion of the adolescent journey. Not only the youth but the entire community suffers. "Because of the unhappy loss of this kind of initiatory experience, the modern world suffers a kind of spiritual poverty and a lack of community," says West African educator Malidoma Somé (1994, p. 68). "Young people are feared for their wild and dangerous energy, which is really an unending longing for initiation."

Three Passages

In our modern world, young people's experience with adolescence is profoundly different from that of former times. In today's U.S. culture, teenagers experience not one but several "passages":

1. The major transformation at puberty when they are awakened from childhood into adolescence.

2. A challenging transition as they leave middle school and enter high school.

3. The "senior passage"—when students step over the threshold out of high school and into adulthood.

Each of these is a time of enormous transition—not only for the student, but also for family and faculty. On the threshold of the unknown, students in transition must say good-bye not only to relationships with others, but to a childhood self—and for older teens, an adolescent identity. Anxiety is normal during these profound changes. Mood swings are common among both the students and parents who feel the shock of letting go. Family relationships may become volatile—familiar patterns between parent and child often change and even reverse, bringing much confusion in their wake. As the child struggles with a new identity, parents need to find new ways to guide this young person who is no longer a child but not mature enough to be on his own.

Middle and high school teachers may feel undermined by students' restlessness, loss of interest in school, or general sense of upheaval. Among high school seniors, even the most disciplined may lose their capacity for focus at this time. This "senioritis" can affect both the quality of learning and the climate between student and teacher. Those who have not had the benefit of an initiation process in their last year of high school are still sorely in need of such an experience as freshmen in college. Does the extremely high national freshman attrition rate (Brawer, 1996) have something to do with our young people being unprepared for the real challenges of leaving the nest?

Just over the brink into her adult life, a college freshmen paints a vivid portrait of the "ordinary trauma" of moving from adolescence to adulthood:

> I seem to have become somewhat lost amidst all of the craziness that college life entails, and I so desperately need to be reminded of who I am. These past few months away from home and all of those whom I love has forced me to grow and change in ways I never deemed possible. I feel more independent and capable than ever...and more alone.
>
> I am the one who has the task of picking myself up when I am down, I am the one who is responsible for pushing myself onward when all I want to do is give up, and I am the one who must wipe my tears away after crying for hours. My parents are no longer only footsteps away, and the friends that I've had for the past 18 years of my life are no longer just around the corner.
>
> I have finally entered into the world on my own, and the eagerness I once felt about this passage has transformed into fear. No, I don't wish that I weren't where I am in my life, nor would I trade the experiences that I've endured for anything. . . . I guess I just

> never realized how much I would come to miss my "old life" once it was gone.

> I love the University . . . and know that it is the right place for me, but it's not home yet, and I really enjoy all of those I've met here, but they aren't my closest friends yet.

> I miss Senior Rites of Passage and wish more than anything that I could once again feel the support, understanding, and identification that I did when I was surrounded by those who formed our incredible group. The memories created in our time together feed the fire that keeps me warm while I'm away.

This young woman is one of the lucky ones—accepted by the college of her choice; provided with funds to go to that college; and blessed with the resilience, skills, and perspective to grapple successfully with her challenges. How much more loneliness and confusion would we find in those who have left high school without all these resources?

Along with turmoil and loss, adolescents also experience an exciting awakening. Students begin to glimpse the possibility of larger purpose and deeper meaning in their lives and in life itself. They begin to ask, and have insight about, the larger questions of existence and human relations. Seniors, and sometimes even younger high school students, begin to have the acuity of mind of the adult while still bubbling with the vitality, playfulness, and humor of the child.

Especially during puberty and the "senior passage," students have the energy, yearnings, and wondering that accompany spiritual awakening. Often dismissed as "hormones," these powerful longings need to be met and channeled so young people can express them in relatively safe ways. Without appropriate support, this awakening can clearly lead to fragility: Potentially creative energies are thwarted into depression or violence. When caring and creative adults in the community really listen to young people and guide them through these passages, students blossom with character, compassion, and the capacity to make positive decisions.

Contemporary Models Within the Broader Community

Some families and ethnic communities have recognized the needs of their children for initiation and have sought after-school approaches. Religious or community rites provide a structure that strengthens the youth as an individual and as a member of that religious or ethnic community. Ceremonies that grow out of a cultural tradition—like the Mexican *Quinceañera* or African American rites of passage—offer a sense of belonging to that particular community with its own values and codes of behavior. In the *Quinceañera,* the girl chooses 14 boys and 14 girls to be part of her ceremony. Along with two adult sponsors, her *madrina* and *padrino,* these peers become a network of support that is meant to last well beyond the actual ceremony.

Speaking of the tribal initiation of his teenage son, a Native American father in my community explained: "He knows who he is; he knows he belongs; we are no longer concerned he will make poor choices." Addressing a group of guidance counselors, this father explained that initiation was designed to clarify the "purpose and meaning of life and what you want to do with your life."

In the Jewish tradition, the *Bar* or *Bat Mitzvah* brings together the scattered families in a celebration of joy, spirit, and ceremony. The enormous preparation and responsibility of leading a portion of the Sabbath service gives the young person confidence and an awareness of the role of sacrifice in worthwhile accomplishment. After his *Bar Mitzvah,* a young boy is eligible to be counted as an adult member of the community.

Other families seek initiation for their children through wilderness challenge programs. Wrenched from the comforts of home, tested and challenged to transcend perceived limits and experience the majesty and ruthlessness of the wilderness, young people often discover personal strength at these critical transition times. My husband and I sent each of our sons off at the age of 14, during the transition from middle to high school, to a program called Educo in the Rocky Mountains. We knew that the program showed a deep understanding of rites of passage. One son went from poor grades and no discipline in middle school to a rigorous focus and straight *A*s his first semester of a challenging high school. When we asked him about his shift, he said:

> I think it happened on Educo. There was that day we first had to climb a fourteener[1] with a heavy pack. I hated every moment of that hike. I was hot and tired and miserable. But when we reached the top, the view was awesome. I had never seen such beauty, never felt so proud. I saw that the work was worth it. I felt it; I saw the results with my own eyes.

Yet most of our youth do not have these opportunities. And those who do may have difficulty bringing what they learned from those experiences into their own school community. In contrast, *school-based programs* offer meaningful initiation experiences to all the students in

---

[1]A "fourteener" is a mountain over 14,000 feet high.

its community. These programs can range from a semester-long course to an integration of methods and coming-of-age themes into an academic class, to an intensive workshop on a school-sponsored retreat. Freshman orientation programs can also be a valuable opportunity for positive initiation experiences. Chip Wood (interview, 1999) notes that disturbing practices, such as freshman hazing, still flourish in communities where no such school-based, authentic initiation is provided. "If the adults don't create a constructive initiation, the kids will find their own, often distorted and destructive, rituals."

Through a rite of passage program at school, students can reflect on their own identity and create an authentic community with other students from across the lines of class, cliques, and gender. Engaging parents, community members, and other educators, such programs create a network of support that strengthens both students and the community.

What Is a Rite of Passage?

Drawing from the essential elements of initiation rites, let's use the following framework to define rites of passage. A rite of passage is . . .

- a structured process
- *guided by adults* in which young people are helped to
- become *conscious about the irrevocable transition* they're in,
- given *tools* for making transitions and separations,
- *initiated* into the *new capacities* required for their next step, and
- *acknowledged* by the community of adults, as well as their peers, for their courage and strength in taking that step.

School-Based Models

Several initiation models exist in education today. This chapter describes two I am personally familiar with.

- *The Senior Passage Course*—a one-semester curriculum for high school seniors that several schools have implemented, some for more than 15 years, in diverse settings ranging from big city private schools to inner-city and small-town public schools.[2]

---

[2]Originally called the senior "Mysteries" course, the Senior Passages Course was created by Jack Zimmerman and later refined by collaborative teams I have worked with at several schools. Since its origination in 1983 at the Crossroads School in Santa Monica, California, I have helped introduce this curriculum successfully in an inner-city high school in the Bronx; to a public high school in Oregon; and as an after-school program in Boulder, Colorado.

• *The ROPE program* (Rites of Passage Experience)—a year-long program for 8th grade students implemented in many U.S. public schools.

The Senior Passage Course

This course provides many ways to address the concerns that arise for graduating seniors, allowing students to see the commonality and normality of their concerns. The 16-week curriculum guides students to recognize and honor the change that is taking place. Students prepare for the impending losses—the loss of childhood, friends, mentors, family, and home town if they are moving away. They learn skills for coping with stress and for making decisions about the future that can minimize stress. New skills, experiences, and attitudes help students create satisfying relationships in the new environments they will enter after graduation.

The course is designed to meet once a week for one and a half or two hours. A retreat is held at least three weeks before the end of the class, like the one attended by Felicia in the opening of this book. The principles and practices for "honoring young voices" outlined in Chapter 1 form the basic methodology for this class—building a safe environment, posing questions about each student's "mysteries," listening to each other's concerns, playing and using symbolic expression; going on adventures, and participating in "councils." Many of the stories and questions from students that you have read in preceding chapters come from this program.

The class begins with building a safe community. Students begin to speak about what is most important to them right now. Then we journey back into their roots—learning about their parents and ancestry, recalling important moments in childhood. The intention is to honor childhood as part of letting it go. Students interview parents and share what feels appropriate. They tell stories about their own names and how those names connect them to their ancestors or people they love. They share a precious memory from childhood.

We encourage seniors to consciously sift and sort through their past, choosing what they want to carry with them and what are "childish ways." At the end of the course, on the retreat, we return to this process of letting go. Back in class, we look toward the future. Themes for councils and dialogues embrace the whole student as we explore issues of body, mind, spirit, emotions, and relationships. Here are a few issues the group considers as they get ready to leave high school:

• What does it feel like now to know you will soon be leaving friends, family and school behind? To be making decisions about your next step?

• However you define the word "spirit," tell us a story about a time when your spirit was nourished.

• To the extent that you know something about your life purpose or destiny, what do you know? What have been the clues? If you don't know, how does that feel?

• How can we understand our yearnings for intimacy—with friends, family, romantic relationships? How has our culture confused sensuality with sexuality, sexuality with intimacy? How do we set goals and boundaries to create what will really nourish us?

Before the retreat, we offer students a framework for understanding rites of passage—a minilesson from anthropology that helps them understand their experience in terms of the universal, archetypal journey all adolescents take to become adults. This framework (see the section "Curriculum vs. Transformation" in this chapter) also gives them tools for constructively navigating other life transitions, as they marry, become parents, make fundamental career shifts, encounter midlife issues, or face aging.

The retreat design diverges widely among the different schools who offer this curriculum. It always includes some time alone to reflect on what students are ready and willing to let go of and what new goals, qualities, or perspective on life they want to call on as they go forward. The group creates a ritual that is responsive to and respectful of that particular group of students and their family traditions. These rituals—in a highly focused, symbolic drama—allow students to honor everything they are letting go of and to declare their strength for future endeavors.

Either just before or after the retreat, some of the Senior Passage programs host an evening for parents and students together. Some programs also host a ceremony for the faculty to honor each graduating senior. At such ceremonies, these "elders" have an opportunity to congratulate the seniors on their growth and welcome the young people into the adult community.

The last three weeks of the course are devoted to helping students integrate what they have learned on their retreat into their ordinary lives. Students practice a variety of tools for positive, constructive good-byes, which they can also use in their other relationships.

ROPE—the Rite of Passage Experience

In sharp contrast to the social and emotional focus of most Senior Passage Courses, ROPE is a highly academic design. A concept originally developed by the Walden III school of Racine, Wisconsin, teachers have used ROPE in middle schools in New Mexico and Colorado, as well. The common thread in these programs is a sequence of 15-minute ceremonies for each individual student at the end of 8th grade. In front of their parents, teachers, peers and representatives from the community, students present a brief portfolio of what they consider to be their best work and then address a common critical-thinking problem to demonstrate their progress both academically and socially.

From the beginning of the year, the 8th grade faculty coach students to prepare for this momentous event. Together, the teachers and students develop procedures for helping students evaluate and refine their own work and gather feedback from parents, peers, and faculty to improve work so their portfolio will ultimately reflect their best efforts. Through the portfolio process, students highlight and hone academic skills deemed essential to success in high school. Students develop presentation, communication, and decision-making skills that will serve them not only in high school, but as a strong springboard for their future. The academic and career-oriented skills offered by ROPE are undoubtedly essential to the passage from childhood to adolescence, from middle to high school. But is this enough? What about deeper needs and desires of young teenagers?

Colleen Conrad's ROPE curriculum addresses these needs. At Conrad's school, the program exists only within the English curriculum. A core question—"What am I now prepared to contribute to society?"—is the focal point for the entire 8th grade English curriculum. Conrad guides this exploration through four major units: an in-depth autobiography, bias and discrimination, poetry, and "man's inhumanity to man (interview, 1999)."

Autobiography. Through their autobiography, students identify their own qualities and abilities. After reading stories from ethnic literature, they research the country of their ancestors. For many of Conrad's students, it is their own birthplace—Mexico, Mongolia, Armenia, Turkey. They explore why their name was chosen and then do a large piece on their family. For Conrad,

> Their autobiography is like a family heirloom they're creating for themselves and their children—I encourage them to put in what they always want to remember so they can teach their children about themselves and where they come from.

Antibias. In the antibias unit, the students begin to develop their own worldview and talk about what kind of difference they can make. First they watch a moving video called "The Power of One," which stimulates discussion about how one person can make a difference. After reading works by Martin Luther King, Jr., they write their own "I have a dream" speech. Conrad invites Vista volunteers to talk about the impact that even kids can make on a community.

The students also create a "peace journal." As the class explores different societies, they struggle to create a worldview that doesn't require physical might and violence to solve problems. After much reading, writing, presenting, and discussing, each student designs a "personal belief statement." The purpose of this statement is to publicly declare how the student intends to view and treat others.

Poetry. Through the poetry unit, Conrad takes them back to the personal level—to explore deeply who they are, how they relate to their world, where they get their sense of identity. They read poems from many different cultures and then write one of that same type, dealing with themes like ethnic pride, important elders, fear, disappointment, anger, and celebrations.

Then they go back to their core question. "In light of all these emotions you've written about and knowing that you can make a difference," asks Conrad, "how can you take all those feelings—pride, anger, fear—and connect them to the fact that you have the personal power to have an impact?"

"Man's Inhumanity to Man." In this final unit, literature and video take students through the Holocaust, the history of native people in Mexico who lost self-governance to European settlers, and the plight of migrant workers and people who are physically or mentally disabled. They talk about places in their own town where inhumanity is practiced, bringing examples from the newspapers and the evening news and tying these stories to the novels, stories, and essays they have read.

Their last major composition before their rites of passage responds to this question: "In light of everything you've learned, do you feel you have a personal responsibility to stand up and oppose inhumanity in the world?"

"Do they ever say no?" I ask Conrad.

"Sometimes. Sometimes they say, 'I'm an American, I have certain privileges, and I don't need to worry about all this.' But 95 percent say, 'I may not change the world, but I can make a difference.'"

Conrad describes the culmination of all their efforts:

> Putting all of these pieces together—the autobiography, their dream, their poetry, their awareness of the world—we ask them to come up with a practical plan of how they can influence their community. Our idea of rites of passage is that part of becoming a young adult is taking responsibility for the world we live in.

When students respond to the core question, they choose to do so in their own way. Selena projected herself into the main characters from each of the books on inhumanity, claiming something from each of them that she felt would prepare her to make her contribution:

> If I could take something from Elie Weisel in *Night* and put it into my life so I could make a difference, I would take his strength and his hope. He never gave up. I could use those qualities. Then I could believe that a change can happen. I can believe that one person can make a difference.

> If I could take something from George in *Of Mice and Men,* I would take his absolute loyalty and love. Then I could make a difference in the lives of people that matter to me and be as fierce and protective of them as he was of his friend.

A powerful transition for the students, this program also infuses the whole school community with a sense of pride and celebration. Faculty from the other subjects do everything in their power to support the presentations. Working parents often take time off from work and bring all the little brothers and sisters and grandma and grandpa, as well.

And for Conrad, this program that came to her late in her career has been a source of immense satisfaction:

> The most important thing ROPE has done for me as a teacher has been to give me a purpose for what I'm doing. It's the principle that unites it all. I have a map for the entire year, I know where we're headed. It's as if each unit I teach is a step along the way, and I know the destination is their rite of passage.

In the ROPE program, we can see many elements of positive initiation:

• The responsibility taken by teachers to prepare their students for a new awareness;

• The tools and capacities;

• The ceremonial presentation where the community honors the students as they culminate an ordeal and cross the threshold from childish ways to a more responsible and capable adolescence.

In the Senior Passage Course, we see these same elements, even though the content is not primarily academic but social, emotional, and spiritual.

Curriculum vs. Transformation—
A Framework for a Comprehensive Rite of Passage

> Change is inevitable, growth is optional.
>
> —ANONYMOUS

A true rite of passage is something more than the acquisition of knowledge or skills. It is more than recognition by elders for preparing for the next phase of life.

To truly meet the soul's hunger for initiation, there must be another element, another tone to the experience. The learning that takes place in a meaningful rite of passage is not simply cognitive growth but changes to the core—"to change the inmost nature of the neophyte, impressing him, as a seal impresses wax, with the characteristics of his new state" (Turner, 1987, p. 11). Or, as anthropologist Colin Turnbull (1983, p. 82) puts it, initiation evokes "the magic of transformation, as distinct from mere transition."

As educators designing a meaningful passage program for our students, how can we foster the magic of transformation and not settle for simply assisting a transition? A series of lesson plans, a well-designed curriculum is not enough.

Each team of educators (and parents) will choose to create the rites of passage program that feels most appropriate for their school community. Possibilities include emotional intensity, ritual and retreat at one end of the spectrum and in-school, academically driven programs at the other. But as you invent or adapt your own design, you can infuse that design with metaphors, symbols, and emotional experiences that speak to the souls of adolescents.

The archetypal images that capture this tone can best be understood through a common structure underlying virtually all rites of passage. (Foster & Little 1987, pp. 89–107):

- Severance (or separation)
- Threshold (or the "in-between" phase)
- Reincorporation (or reentry)

Through this framework of meaning, educators can design a curriculum appropriate to the age group and the particular classroom community.

It might be an additional course, such as Senior Passages or a 9th grade "Transitions" course. In English, it might involve a curriculum like Conrad's, or it might use the unifying theme of "coming of age" literature. Doug Eaton (interview, 1999) integrates the Senior Passage curriculum into a science elective called "Society and Nature," which weaves together an exploration of identity, community, and geology and also meets district character education standards. Or a school may integrate the theme and process of initiation into the entire curriculum for one grade level, such as some of the ROPE programs. Some schools begin by designing these elements primarily into a retreat.

Severance

Severance announces the end of one way of being and the beginning of another. In a rite of passage, severance has two primary functions. First is *separating* from what you have known, what is familiar and secure. In some metaphoric, ceremonial way, guides take the young people away from their homes, parents, and community. The initiates are encouraged to say good-bye and to understand that in loss, we make room for something new to come in.

The second function is about *letting go* of aspects of yourself that no longer serve you. To sever means "to cut away": We encourage students to prune away qualities or habits or ways of relating that may have been useful in our younger days but now hold us back.

Recognizing Fear. Both of these tasks evoke fear. Acknowledging this fear releases essential fuel for the journey. Teachers can give their students assignments that allow them to reflect on what they want to let go of, how they feel about being wrenched out of the comfort zone of childhood, and what fears emerge as they embark on this journey. Many of our students have been taught that to become strong, they must conquer fear. We can offer an alternative: Fear can become an ally—a scout for danger and source of courage—when we learn how to relate to it with honesty.

Storyteller Laura Simms (1998) celebrates the value of fear:

> Fear is not to be avoided, repressed or conquered. For from the very depths of fear itself arises fearlessness, awareness and wisdom. The acknowledgment and experience of fear is the door that opens us to heightened presence and perception through which we learn to live in the world as it is (p. 46).

As we invite students to share their fears and how they work with their fear, we often see other perspectives emerge—and sometimes students express their religious views: "I take my fear and my confusion to

God." Or, as another student reflected: "I was scared to go on this solo—I don't like being alone, and right now I am so confused about which college to choose. It's hard to be alone with all this pressure on me. So I prayed a lot. It's hard to take so much time to pray at home—I was so glad to have this time to pray."

Designing a Ritual. Severance can be accelerated through the intensity and symbolic dramatization of ritual. Some teachers invent rituals of separation. In our program, we invite students to create and enact their own rituals of severance.

On the first day of our retreat, students are divided into small groups who go off into separate rooms to design their ritual.

One group began by leading the entire class in a group hug—a huddle that students saw as a metaphor for being a part of something, for the comfort and safety of community. Kaley Warner (personal communication, 1998) described the rest in her journal:

> Then we slowly broke away and headed off by ourselves where we experienced loneliness and the severing that is surely coming. We meditated upon our fears, we let them consume us, we knew them and acknowledged their presence in us. I dwelt on my fear of loneliness, my fear of being in a new place, alone, starting over.
>
> I thought about judgments. I'm afraid of others' thoughts; I'm afraid of my own. Whose standards am I striving to meet? Is there a perfection out there? These fears, these questions about me, about the universe, the future, people, now. . . .

Another group created a ritual in which they used square knots (which hold tighter the more they're pulled) and slip knots (which release easily with a simple yank) to symbolize friendships that endure and those that fade. Kaley Warner responded in her journal:

> I wonder which relationships in my life are slip knots. Which people will disappear when I pull on my rope to explore the "end of my line" beyond where my leash allows me to travel? Who is a square knot? Who, when I pull, will be solid and strong? With whom will I still have a connection, a bond, after we travel opposite ways? (Warner, personal communication, 1998).

These two rituals suggest the range of metaphors students create when they are free to choose and invent collaboratively. Not all groups bring this serious focus to the task. Some are more playful, easing their awkwardness with ritual through laughter and even cynicism. As mentors, we welcome both, acknowledging that each individual, each group is free to make their own choices about the place of ritual in their lives.

Death Imagery and Severance. Death imagery is central to severance, or separation. Whether consciously or subconsciously, people at times of radical transitions in their lives often experience sudden fears, fascinations, or yearnings about death. Some of this ideation comes simply because death (and rebirth) is the most potent symbol of what we feel when our identity is undergoing an irrevocable change.

Death imagery is common in the dreams, poems, and even personal disclosures of adolescents. When we come across this imagery, as teachers, we must sensitively determine in dialogue with the student whether this is suicidal ideation or is about metaphoric meaning. In the poetry and autobiographies of her students in preparation for ROPE, Colleen Conrad each year discovers images of suicide and abuse. After describing her careful, step-by-step follow-up with one of these students, Conrad explained why she takes these disclosures seriously:

> When my own son was in 8th grade, he made a serious suicide attempt. He was hospitalized, and we knew he would be in long-term care and not going back to school. When I went to school to clean his locker, I found a poetry journal that had been graded by the teacher. It was full of clues about his suicide attempt.
>
> I went to the teacher. I was so upset. "Why wasn't I called?" I asked. "Why didn't you let me know."
>
> "I don't ever take those things seriously," was all she said.
>
> I always take these things seriously now. Because it was so close to home, I saw what can happen. I realize that sometimes kids write about death and are not really planning anything. But I never take that chance.

For years, I noticed a melancholy in certain 7th or 8th grade girls which, when given a safe way to express it, was sometimes confided in statements such as "I wonder why I keep thinking about death, dreaming about it, too. I really don't want to die—but it just keeps coming up." I knew that adolescents often grieve the loss of their childhood—which can seem like "dying" to them. Their current sense of loss can also bring up forgotten, unhealed grief. But why the girls? One year, I glimpsed an answer in a "women-only" council during a senior retreat:

> I used to feel so free. I didn't have to wear shirts. I could look like a boy, act like a boy, and have all the freedom that boys have. I mean, now I see that there are some good things, some great and

beautiful things about being a woman that I cherish. I'm ready for them now, I think. But back then, it was like I died. Like the body, the self that I was so used to, that was me, was gone—gone forever and I was someone else that I couldn't even begin to figure out. I didn't ask for that change, you know. It just happened to me. It just hit me, out of the blue. It was awful.

Giving students an opportunity to tell these stories, express these feelings, and reflect on the meaning of death both as a metaphor and as a reality can provide much comfort for the adolescent in transition. "Understanding the significance of death in the process of transformation and proceeding from there to define one's priorities in life are important aspects of becoming an adult," says David Oldfield, whose "Journey" program has been implemented worldwide (cited in McCullough, 1996, p. 50).

In giving up a childhood self, the adolescent glimpses the first of many little "deaths" that will occur throughout the life cycle. A rite of passage helps adolescents face this loss consciously, in an environment safe enough to express a range of feelings from grief to exhilaration. As a result, the young person discovers a world of resources within and beyond the self.

Threshold

Also called the "liminal" phase, this is the in-between place of *limbo* in our own development when we are no longer rooted in our old self but have not yet discovered or consolidated a new self. Key elements of threshold are:

• Adventure or ordeal
• Choice and responsibility
• Becoming open to new perspectives on life and personal meaning

The word *threshold* refers to a plank at the base of a door; it also implies a sifting and sorting action (threshing) that separates the valuable from the worthless, the "wheat from the chaff." Threshing will allow the young person—the initiate—to know what to leave behind and what to take along, over the threshold, into adulthood. As part of threshing, we sort out, keep, and celebrate what is still good about the past.

Celebrating the past is part of completion, which helps us let go and move on. Giving birth to a new self, students sort out their own values, goals, and relationships with others: Who are my true friends?

Which attachments support bad habits, and which are worthy of on-going commitment? Ultimately, this sifting helps young people recognize the adult principle of active choice in taking responsibility for their own life.

Adventure or Ordeal. As part of this limbo world-between-worlds, young people wrestle with fear and loneliness and face challenges that take the initiate beyond perceived limits. Through this adventure, or "ordeal," the young person discovers the courage, perseverance, and compassion essential to adult life. Tried and tested, going beyond the comfort and apparent security of childhood, the initiate often discovers new sources of power within or beyond the self.

The ordeal may take the form of a physical challenge—such as a ropes course, rock climbing and rappelling. In ROPE, young people face the academic "ordeal" of persevering through setbacks to create and publicly present their best work and authentic vision. Doug Eaton (interview, 1999) takes his students on a long, steep hike that follows a raging river. In other programs, it may come through the quiet receptivity of solitude and stillness.

Not all students are ready at the same time to face a particular challenge. And an activity that challenges one student in a meaningful way may either be so simple that it is meaningless, or so frightening that teachers or peers must help them find other meaningful challenges.

The greatest challenge for most students is to learn how to let go of the shame of not feeling good enough. Although we encourage students to test their limits, to do things they didn't believe possible, we always emphasize that they need to be true to themselves, and kind and gentle to themselves in the process.

Choice and Responsibility. Another aspect of this ordeal is proving yourself worthy of the trust and respect of your community. The initiate demonstrates the physical skills, the knowledge, values, ethics, and spiritual strength that mark adulthood in their community. For some young people who have had a troubled or trouble-making past, coming through a difficult ordeal may earn them the right to ask their community to wipe the slate clean and allow them to create a new identity.

Perhaps the most dramatic transformation I witnessed in a student came not from conquering fears or physical challenges, but from being willing and able to shed the hatred she felt toward herself and others. As Leah wrote in a letter:

> Remember all those times I said I hated everyone at my high
> school and that none of them were worth my time? Well, sud-

denly, I didn't hate anyone anymore. That's one of the things I learned has impacted me the most—that we are all the same. We all have fears and pains and some good sides and some bad sides. I judged people so easily before, I felt hate so easily. Senior Passage showed me a whole new way to look at people. I discovered the beauty of an open mind.

Leah had learned not only to let go of hatred towards others but towards herself. She came into our class originally with a look that clearly reflected a deep self-loathing. As she began to take in the affection of the group, and particularly after the deep connection of the retreat, Leah began to radiate beauty and confidence.

Being Open to New Perspectives. Often the result of the initiation ordeal is a new vision for one's life:

I was sitting alone up in a high place overlooking this little canyon, and I asked the question about what to do next year: Do I go to college or take a year off? I've been so confused about this for months. It was startling then to get such a clear response. It was as if nature or the universe was telling me so clearly what to do.

Everything became crystal clear; I was just sitting back and listening. I came back down feeling so fulfilled, so happy, realizing what I wanted to do.

You know, there are so many minutes and hours when I'm alone inside. But there's something about going into nature, going without any plan that sparks this new awareness in me.

At the threshold, students begin to discover and articulate a new framework of meaning—a new perspective on what is important, a clarity of purpose from which it becomes possible to set meaningful goals and make choices that serve their larger sense of mission.

Before discussing reentry, I want to probe more deeply into the meaning and value of the ordeal in rites of passage.

Ordeal

I am not sure whether the initiation to the next level in life's journey can take place without an ordeal. And it is an ordeal to let go of our old ways. As outworn and inadequate as the "old self" may be, it is familiar. To abandon security for the unknown is terrifying, and we resist facing that terror as long as possible.

The ordeal plunges us into that terror. In my own transitions, I have often felt that I was "losing my way," "losing faith," or "losing my balance" before I was ready to release my attachment to one way of life and cross the threshold into another.

When I have crossed, a peace descends into my heart. My mind can look back and grasp the insights available from this new perspective. But to get across, I must face the fear, confusion, and self-doubt that are the essence of the ordeal. At last, the "old self" gives up and leaves an open space for something new to emerge.

For adolescents, going through an initiation ordeal can be unbearable without the support of committed, caring adults. The "ordeal" phase of the rite of passage for our students can have many profoundly different tones and flavors. It begins with something we elders structure—teachers can create a "curriculum," a "lesson plan," a "strategy" for challenging the student. Chip Wood (interview, 1999) cautions that adolescents are already so filled with fear that, as educators, we must be extremely careful if we inadvertently make them more fearful.

For the 8th grade students in the Fort Collins ROPE program, the ordeal is a series of academic projects accompanied by self-examination, feedback from others, and continual improvement—leading ultimately to a brief, intense, comprehensive public performance. For high school seniors with whom I have worked, the initiation ordeal is a period of solitude and a series of intense councils that invite students to speak out about their fears, their untold suffering, and their passionate yearnings. For seniors in the Bronx, the ordeal comes simply with spending much of a day alone in a natural setting that is completely alien to the crowded streets and tenements they know so well.

As I stated previously, the ordeal "begins" with something we structure. By our planned activity, and the spirit and tone with which we offer that activity, we show our empathy with adolescents, who have most likely been undergoing their own private ordeals. Even the simplest and most abbreviated form of ordeal can allow a student to concentrate months and even years of yearning and struggling to face what needs to be faced and experience a profound release. I have seen 18-year-olds turn a 45-minute "solo" into a life-altering encounter with their deepest fears, with astonishing insight, or with opening up to whatever they consider to be their higher power.

This is the power of ritual. In the safety of a ritual activity and a community that we have carefully co-created with our students, we offer a symbolic expression of a struggle and challenge that might never be resolved in daily life. Through metaphor and drama, students enact precisely the ordeal and release for which their souls are yearning.

Reentry or Incorporation

The real challenge of a rite of passage is to integrate new insights, new patterns of behavior, and a new identity back into ordinary life. "If our withdrawal from the world does not prepare us for our reentry into the world, then our whole quest has been in vain" (Kamperidis, 1992, p. 16).

Many people who work with youth have had little or no awareness of the challenge of reentry. Schools often plan intense retreats to culminate the year. Nonschool programs take students into the wilderness (or out of the country) for a potentially life-changing experience and then say good-bye as the young people drop back into a life where no one understands what they have been through. No one helps them as they try to integrate such dizzying new awarenesss into a lifestyle that pulls them back toward all their old ways. When students are not adequately prepared for and supported through reentry, they can be easily hurt; and they can lose much of what they have learned. There are two dimensions of reentry: the preparation for reentry while still on the journey and the reentry experience itself.

Preparing for Reentry. As part of the closing of any identity-altering retreat, it is crucial to take time to prepare for reentry. A solid closure gives students an opportunity to discuss what they have gained and how they feel about going home. The adolescents can thus consolidate new insights or commitments by sharing them in front of caring adults and peers. Formalizing the act of saying good-bye to this special time and place also brings a sense of completion and strength.

Preparation also means anticipating what may occur when they return. Because most youth have no way to imagine some of the pitfalls, teachers can offer scenarios like these.

• You might feel disoriented. Be careful when you first drive—the speed and noise may seem overwhelming after slowing down so dramatically.

• Your parents and friends will ask you what you "did," or what "happened." You may find yourself unable to find the words—or that simply describing activities can't possibly show what you now feel inside. Find a kind way to tell your loved ones that you hope your behavior will show what you learned on the retreat.

• Your criteria for friendships may change. You may find yourself reevaluating who you want to be with now. You may also find yourself sliding into precisely the old patterns you resolved to change. You may lose the feeling of exuberance, faith, or invincibility you may have experienced after coming through your ordeal. You might even feel depressed or cynical about whether any of this "new identity" stuff or "sense of community" is real.

Back at School. In the Senior Passage Course, we allow at least three class sessions after a retreat to process the reentry feelings and to carefully say our good-byes. Lyla wrote this about reentry:

> I did not enjoy reentry into a world full of hate, judgment, biases, lack of communication, misunderstandings, and an absence of full supportiveness. I'm not saying that I never engage in any of these elements, but they can be very depressing. When you are immersed in a loving, supportive environment, like on our retreat, it's hard not to be caught up in that attitude. Well, the same logic applies to an environment full of the previously mentioned negative attitudes.

In our dialogues with students in the closing hours or weeks of a Passage course, we remind them that this experience is not only for themselves but for the renewal of their community. They have *received* a gift—the priceless opportunity of going on a retreat—and usually they have an intense awareness of this privilege; and now they must find a way to *give* a gift. To symbolize this gift the students will bring back to the community, we often encourage students to create or find some small token that they can bring back with them and give to someone. And we remind them that the gift of a new self speaks louder than words or even the most precious object.

In the second dimension of reentry, the students' elders—both teachers and parents in their community—welcome and honor the young people. In our work with seniors, we have designed two ceremonies that allow adults to welcome the initiates and acknowledge their new adult status.

The Parent Evening. The parent evening is designed both to help the parents let go of their growing children and to allow the students to receive acknowledgments from their parents in front of others. It begins with a playful warm-up and a brief introduction of our purpose. Then we hold a council for both parents and students. First the students speak about what it feels like to be making big decisions and leaving so much behind. The parents listen carefully and then respond briefly.

> "I feel hope for the future for the first time," says one father, jumping up to speak. "I'm a coach; I work with young people all the time, but I never get to hear their innermost thoughts. I can't believe how articulate and wise these kids are!"

> "I knew my son was dealing with these feelings, even though he's reluctant to tell us sometimes," says a mother. "But listening to the same feelings coming from so many students— it helps me understand and appreciate my own son so much better."

Then the parents speak about how they feel about their son or daughter leaving. And looking at a baby picture and at their child today, they comment on the growth they see. Each year, parents and students are profoundly moved by the depth of feeling when parents seize this rare opportunity to publicly honor their own child. Doug Eaton (interview, 1999) writes about a boy for whom no parents could come:

> Kyle lost his mom to cancer in his freshman year, and his father has had health problems and wasn't present. So two mothers who had seen Kyle grow up and play with their own sons tearfully honored his courage and big heart. Kyle beamed and got up and hugged them both.

When the students are asked to speak about what it is like to observe this, many comment about the new respect they feel for adults as they see their honesty, caring, and struggle to be good parents.

The week after parent night, we ask students to speak about the experience. Lydia went first, her eyes twinkling.

> First of all, it was so cool to sit there while my parents were being so proud of me in front of everyone. I mean, I know they love me, but it was really different to have them say all those things in front of everyone. . . . I never thought I'd live to see my dad and my step-dad holding hands. You know, they used to be best friends.

Sometimes the rift that shows up on parent night is between a father and his son, or between both parents and a rebellious daughter. Each year, we watch at least one family, in the love and commitment they bring forth during this ceremony, move—if only for a moment— towards mending their breach.

The Senior Honoring Ceremony. For faculty, we hold another ceremony that helps bring closure and unites the community. In the story that opened Chapter 1, the boy who carried Felicia on his shoulders received an unexpected gift when he returned from that journey. At the ceremony, a teacher spoke to Jimmy in front of the assembled students, parents, and teachers:

"When you came into my class, I could tell that you were used to being one of the clowns. Yet when it came time to share our stories, you took the first risk. You inspired all of us with the courage of your vulnerability. You led the way. And throughout our class, I saw you as a leader—someone who would dare to do things, say things in a new way.

"I have watched you grow this last year and become strong. . . . I know you have been appreciated at this school for the great things you've done on the baseball field, and for the humor you've brought to leaven deadly moments. But I also want to honor you for the warmth you brought to each one of us, and the initiative and courage you've shown—like when you offered to carry Felicia on your shoulders when she was too weak to walk to our ceremony. I respect you as a leader and value you as a friend."

The young man is beaming. Behind him, his father looks stunned. This is the younger son—the cut-up—a disappointment after the academic achiever who went before him. This one has brought the father to the disciplinary dean's office one too many times to allow the father to see much promise in the boy. Now he has listened to one of the most respected teachers in the school describe the outstanding gifts of character his boy has demonstrated in his last year of high school. His face begins to soften, and tears glisten in his eyes. He places his hands on the broad shoulders of his son—one squeeze tells this boy that his father is willing to see him in a new light.

Seen in a new way by his teacher, his peers, and ultimately, his father and the community, this young man's initiation experience not only supported his leap into adulthood but affected others, as well. Rites of passage meet a need in our young people, but they also renew the *community as a whole.* Initiation may transform a girl into a woman, a boy into a man, but it also strengthens the community by adding new adults who have much to contribute—new members who are responsible carriers of the culture (Mahdi, 1996, p. xv). On a more modest scale, our senior honoring ceremonies touch into that experience of traditional cultures, where the community was revitalized by coming together in joyous celebration.

‰ ‰ ‰

When I first heard Malidoma Somé speak about initiation in 1995, I was moved to tears when he spoke about reentry. I try to recapture his words when I speak to the parents of my students about the importance of welcoming and honoring their students after their ordeal. This accomplished West African educator and author said, "You Americans are always trying to initiate yourselves into adulthood." He went on to startle us with words like these:

Because no one gave you this gift, you try to initiate yourself.

Over and over again, you put yourself through ordeals—divorce, major illnesses, accidents, career losses, and major moves.

You keep stretching yourself to become stronger, to heal your wounds.

And you do it. You succeed. You make a leap and you become so much more responsible, so much more mature.

But then no one welcomes you back. No tribe of elders are there for you to bless you and recognize that, in the eyes of the community, you are grown up.

And so you have to do it again. It is as if it never happened.

Because you are not welcomed, you have to do it again and again.

If we can give our young people the tools, if we can challenge them in constructive ways to let go and choose growth, perhaps this next generation will not always need to learn "the hard way." Of course, life will always present us with loss, pain, and even betrayal. But if these young people learn how to navigate change, how to cultivate transformation, perhaps we can help them avoid unnecessary loneliness and suffering. When young people are guided and welcomed by mentors, the experience of the initiation journey will guide them through life's many transitions.

Conclusion

From Fear to Dialogue—From Standoff to Collaboration

Defining the "moral meaning" of democracy, John Dewey (1957) wrote that "the supreme task of all political institutions . . . shall be the contribution they make to the all-round growth of every member of society" (p. 186). If we are educating for wholeness, for citizenship, and for leadership in a democracy, *spiritual development belongs in schools.*

Just imagine if every student in the United States were provided a safe place to sit with a small group of their peers and reflect on their lives . . . to share the questions that trouble or confuse or mystify them . . . to find support for their pain or joy . . . to discover the solace that comes in silence . . . to be challenged to respect those who appear to be fundamentally different from them.

Making such experiences available to every student could be an effective strategy for preventing violence and other social pathologies. Such experiences not only nourish students' spiritual development, they also help them transcend prejudice, increase academic motivation, improve focus and cooperation, foster creativity, and keep more kids in school. In other words, *caring about the inner lives of our students makes educational sense at every level.*

This book is an invitation to remember what we already know: The connection among souls is ultimately what education is about. There is no single right way to do it, no blueprint. But there are paths to the souls of students that are open to every teacher, in every classroom, in every school. All we need is the courage to walk these paths with our students.

Traveling through the seven gateways to the soul of students—through connection, silence, meaning, joy, creativity, transcendence, and initiation—we found many opportunities for honoring the yearnings of young people. In their poignant stories and profound questions, in their desperate acts of violence and self-destruction, our students express their longing for something more—for something deeper than ordinary, fragmented existence.

If this book does nothing more, I hope it reveals the existence of this yearning in our youth and the dramatic rise in wisdom when students can share their quest with one another. Although some families have provided guidance and regular opportunities for their children to address their spiritual hunger, many young people have no safe place to share their inner life. Their parents have been lost or caught up in their own journey. Even if they have been part of the great wave of spiritual renewal in the '90s, many parents have not yet discovered a way to translate appropriately for their children what is so rich and sustaining for them. And even when students have been blessed with a rich inner life at home, they often feel compelled to leave this resource outside school doors.

Many adults have judged this generation of adolescents as shallow, selfish, and vacuous. The wisdom, wonder, and search of young people today often goes unseen or misunderstood beneath all the defenses they have erected to protect their fragility and to express their despair. Whether or not educators and parents are drawn to my suggestions for working with the soul in schools, those who recognize this hunger in the voices of students may discover their own ways to respond to these needs.

I am also eager for teachers to discover new strategies to welcome the inner life and build meaningful connections in the classroom. Some of the examples in this book, such as encouraging students to keep journals, are so simple, so unarguable that educators can incorporate them with ease. But other strategies, and indeed the entire enterprise of welcoming soul into the school, may provoke controversy, fear, and confusion.

Controversy and confusion can divide us—pitting us against one another and preventing us from taking action. For some educators and parents, the teaching strategies suggested here will be considered a violation of private religious beliefs or even a violation of the law—no matter how careful I have been to respect those concerns. Traditionalists may feel that some methods are "New Age" or "relativistic." Secular humanists may be offended at providing the option for prayer or speaking up about a student's faith or religious passion in a classroom. Progressive or holistic educators may feel that the suggestions in these chapters are too limiting and that it is time to provide students with concrete tools and practices for cultivating spiritual growth. Each of these voices represents friends and respected colleagues from whom I have learned a great deal.

Despite their differences, each side has grave concerns about the current state of our youth and is urgently searching for ways to foster connection, meaning, and integrity in our students. I have sought to create this book as a bridge between those who share common goals but have found few forums in which to dialogue together. My goal has been to provide a framework that allows educators to honor, evoke, and nourish the souls of students in ways that do not violate deeply held convictions about the worldview or religion dear to them and their families.

After spending two years in a dialogue group composed of traditionalist Christians and progressive and mainstream educators, I cannot deny the deeply entrenched and fundamental differences of belief that make it seem impossible at times to work together. But when we agree that students must have a place for their yearning to be heard, that our schools can no longer afford to shortchange or shut out the inner life of students, I believe we can transform this controversy into a lively dialogue committed to creating strategies suitable for each community. To be willing to take on this challenge, we must also face our fear.

Acknowledging the Risks

Fear can be a useful guide—it announces dangers that we should heed. But fear can also paralyze us. For decades, educators have allowed fear to keep the spiritual dimension out of our schools. If we can acknowledge this fear and listen carefully to its guidance, perhaps we can also examine our paralysis, respectfully engage our differences, and strive to find some new areas of common ground.

There are indeed great risks in encouraging schools to tend the heart and feed the soul of young people:

• We risk the overzealous teacher, who gets so carried away with wanting to nurture spiritual development that he foists his own personal beliefs on impressionable children.

• We risk the half-hearted teacher who tries to implement "cutting-edge strategies" in a mechanical way that breeds even more cynicism and alienation in our youth.

• We risk parents who feel "dissed" and dismissed by educators who plow ahead with new techniques they naively adopt as "neutral" or "nonreligious" without realizing they reflect and potentially proselytize a worldview directly opposed to what is being taught at home.

• We risk parents who will sue teachers and administrators before they even take the time to find out whether new strategies are really a violation of their beliefs or whether they just fit some preconceived "red flags" not really disrespectful in this situation.

• We risk encountering students who are so cynical or afraid of being thought vulnerable at school that they will disrupt or destroy an accepting environment in the classroom so no one dares speak from the heart.

• We risk unleashing a torrent of dammed-up emotions in students for whom the least invitation to authenticity provides an opening for genuine trauma or attention-seeking melodrama.

The following are some guidelines for teachers on how to deal with our fears about ourselves, our students, and their parents when we consider nurturing spiritual development in public schools.

Teachers: Risk and Opportunity

For teachers to address the spiritual development of students, they must simultaneously cultivate their own. "Deep speaks to deep," says Parker Palmer (1998, p. 31). In training and coaching teachers for 15 years, I have seen that beyond methods and theory, a more elusive quality profoundly affects the learning that is possible—the teacher's own integrity, self-awareness, and capacity to be open.

"In teaching . . . there is a secret hidden in plain sight," writes Palmer (1995). "*Good teaching can never be reduced to technique—good teaching comes from the identity and integrity of the teacher.* The quality of the work that is done . . . depends at least as much (and often more) on the inner qualities of the person doing it as it does on his or her technical skill" (p. 2, emphasis in original). Although this truth holds for any kind of teaching, the messages our students receive from our modeling are even more potent when we invite not only mind and body, but also heart, spirit, and community into our classrooms.

Throughout this book, we saw negative examples of what can happen when the lesson plan is more important than the caring and responsiveness of the teacher. We can have the best available curriculum and train teachers in technique and theory, but if we do not provide opportunities for teachers to develop their own emotional intelligence, their own spiritual depth, our students may still be unsafe and our programs hollow.

"We teach who we are."

"Walk your talk."

Or, as Emerson put it, "What you are speaks so loudly that I can't hear what you say you are."

We as educators can cultivate this elusive quality—what I call "the teaching presence" (Kessler, 1998)—not only in private but in school. Through mentoring programs and carefully designed staff development workshops, teachers can build a safe community among colleagues where they can explore their own feelings and experiences. They can practice and refine the fundamental principles that inform teaching in all of the gateways to soul in education, such as eliciting creativity and joy in students. They can hold their own faculty "council" meetings, write reflectively in their own journals, and "pair" with a colleague to share insights and feelings. In these ways, educators can explore questions and topics like these:

• What gives you a sense of worth or meaning in your life?

• Tell a story about a time when your spirit, whatever that means to you, was nourished.

• Share a precious moment from your own childhood—one that you want never to forget.

• Tell us a story of a teacher or other adult who, by positive or negative example, inspired you to be the kind of teacher you are today.

These questions not only sensitize teachers to their students but also build an ongoing faculty community that supports and renews the inner life of teachers. In addition, creating regular opportunities for silent reflection for teachers can refresh and connect teachers at another level. By practicing silence and reflection ourselves, we learn how to be calm and firm when we introduce this practice to our students.

Whether or not teachers choose to explore their own depths, entering the arena of soul with our students can drop us into a cauldron of our own emotional and spiritual growth. In supervising secondary teachers, in particular, I have watched how issues or wounds not yet examined by a teacher will show up in neon in the mirror of adolescent search and struggle. If we are unwilling to honestly address these personal issues, we can go numb or be rocked off our moorings.

In Chapter 5, I introduced the idea of both teachers and students' exploring qualities or impulses that popular culture or our own families have encouraged us to disown. In my workshops with educators, teachers have been grateful for the opportunity to have safe and private ways to look at what they envy or cannot tolerate in others, what they dare not see in themselves.

We examine together:

• Our discomfort with sadness that makes it hard to be open when students express grief.

• Our confusion about power that may keep us from protecting our students through respectful discipline.

• Our fear of vulnerability that may distance us from students.

• Our awareness of the dangerous border between caring and attraction when discovering the beauty in each student.

When teachers receive such support from colleagues, we can be more open with students and also discern when our own concerns are meant for adult ears only. In Chapter 3, we acknowledged the danger of using our students as our own support group if we are not conscious about our responsibility as elders or if we are so isolated that we have no other place to speak from the heart.

Another dangerous impulse for a teacher committed to working with heart and soul in the classroom is becoming inflated with the fantasy of being a "spiritual guide," or "healer." Our gift as teachers is to help students find their *own* answers, not to claim to know all the answers ourselves. Our power comes in asking what will empower our students and in cultivating our humility and humanity, not our own charisma or indispensability. If we can do this, we will naturally align with the First Amendment's protection of the freedom of our students to pursue their religious liberty while restraining us as public officials from "establishing" or imposing our own worldviews and practices.

The suggestions in this book are only a beginning for teachers and administrators who want to welcome soul into education with safety and integrity. When teachers are nourished and honored by the administrators and parent community that holds them accountable, they are more likely to provide these gifts to their students. Teachers need not only caring and respect but also the time and other resources for training and coaching.

Parents: From Fear to Dialogue

As a teacher, I was surprised how easy it was to fall into an "us versus them" mentality with parents. As educators, we have often separated ourselves from parents out of fear that they would criticize us for not being good enough for their "darlings." Then, as a parent, when my own children entered high school, I was surprised at how easily I felt intimidated by teachers who could judge me for not being a good enough parent or who held so much power over the future of my child. Here are some guidelines for working with parents:

• Communicating with parents early and continuously is vital to making a safe place for soul into schools. When we inform parents of new practices, listen and *respond to* their concerns in refining our curriculum and teaching strategies, we are far more likely to provide the respectful climate that allows this work to flourish.

• We can invite parents early in the semester to come for an introductory evening program. Here, parents can listen to an overview and discussion of goals; they can also experience some playful warm-ups and a "council" meeting on a theme that is relevant to them as parents, such as "What is working for you with your teens, and what is most challenging at this stage?" Parents love this opportunity to share with other parents. The methods used with their children become clarified and demystified. And if we find objections among parents to certain practices, we can resolve conflicts together and make decisions that reflect *our* community.

• We can create opportunities later in the year to bridge the gap and strengthen the bonds between students and parents—such as the evening Senior/Parent councils described in Chapter 8 (which, by the way, work in a modified form for other grade levels of secondary schools, as well).

We *must* work with parents because families are the first and most important sources for students' joy, creativity, purpose, and all the other gateways to soul in education. Parents' wisdom and modeling continue to shape these young people throughout their lives. Even when we take students through an initiation process that helps them separate from their parents and become adults, it is clear that students are most successful in becoming adults when there has been a strong foundation from which to launch.

Parent evenings not only help parents support the growth of their own children, but they also help strengthen the adult community essential for soulful approaches to survive in schools. My colleagues and I have watched parents become our allies after parent/student councils or during the Senior Honoring Ceremony. Doug Eaton (interview, 1999) told me with tears in his eyes:

I was so stunned. This dad who had refused to let his daughter attend our overnight trip because he was suspicious of the program made a special trip to see me on his way to work the morning after the parent/student council. He wanted to express his gratitude, and he offered to support me and the program in any way he could.

Working together, teachers and parents become, if only for an evening or a semester, a team of elders collaborating to raise the next generation.

Saboteurs and Kids At Risk

Teachers raise two primary concerns about students when they consider ways to bring heart and soul into the classroom. They fear the students who will go too far and those who will not go far enough. The first type of student is likely to overwhelm the teacher or other students with too much emotion, too many problems. The second refuses to engage, or sabotages the engagement of others with their cynicism and disrespect.

In Chapter 6, we looked carefully at the Pandora's Box question, addressing the students who become "too emotional" in our classes or use our forums to reveal current or threatened violence. These can be the "early warning signs" we are now urgently seeking after the tragedies in Springfield, Padukah, and Littleton. The key here is that teachers trust those colleagues trained to handle psychological problems and make referrals quickly. This, too, is a matter for staff development and for building a strong sense of community among the faculty. Sometimes, we don't really believe our students' threats or eruptions. But such assessments are best made by trained professionals.

What about the students who undermine the value or the feelings of being safe to "speak from the heart" in school? In my experience, they often fall into two camps. One is the verbal, often very intellectual, student who makes an articulate case for why social, emotional, or spiritual development doesn't belong in school; this student often feels offended and is unwilling to participate. The second is the student who says nothing directly to criticize the program but acts out in ways that sabotage the climate of acceptance and safety the group needs. Let's look at strategies for working constructively with these students.

Throughout this book, we have looked at ways to respect the timing and privacy of students. Both the saboteur and the cynic can sometimes be defused by permission to be silent or just to observe. I learned something more from Jack, a well-known cut-up, when he expressed—

in devastating detail—his skepticism about our 10th grade human development class:

"I think this kind of class could get sappy and fake. We could all just pretend to be talking about real feelings, and it would all be a joke. Or we could get real and then go too far. I mean, this is school, you know, it's not therapy; and we could start getting real personal with people's problems and I think that would be a real mistake."

I listened carefully to Jack and felt myself get more and more defensive. His posture said, "I know how to throw you off guard, lady, just like I do everywhere I go." I recognized one of those "negative leaders"—the rebel who influences other students to use jokes and sidetalk and even philosophical debate to disempower teachers. But then, in an instant, I considered another possibility. He was bright and thoughtful—and though I disagreed with him, I appreciated the way he spoke honestly about his skepticism.

Then I spoke in a way I never had: "Jack, I really appreciate your honesty. And I think you're right. All those things *could* happen here if we're not careful. You have an unusual wisdom to be able to see these dangers, and I wonder if you would be willing to take some leadership here in helping our class make sure those things don't happen. And when you see them happening, please let us know."

Jack looked stunned. He was silent for a moment, and I watched his body language change. He sat up tall in his chair, and he said, "I could do that. As a matter of fact, I'd be glad to do that—to help in that way."

And he did. In that moment of being acknowledged and respected, Jack decided to become a leader in our class. He was an ally, almost a partner, for me that year in making the class a success. And the next spring, Jack decided to run for student body president. Our school had always elected juniors for that position to reign during their senior year. That year, after watching a brilliant and unique campaign, the students elected Jack—a sophomore.

The lesson I learned with Jack has infused all my work since then—with teachers and students alike. When I can genuinely consider and acknowledge my critic as a guide—when I can see in their attack, skepticism, or disappointment a needed correction or warning—a critic can indeed become my ally. And the lesson is never lost on the rest of the group.

I learned another lesson after years of confusion and mistakes. For some students who are particularly raw from a recent or ongoing trauma, it can be unbearable to be around students who are sharing openly. Yet it is hard to keep silent when others are speaking. Others can't bear to have their feelings activated at school by a teacher's themes or another student's stories. The more vulnerable students often feel that it is too risky to share their enormous pain in school.

I learned to find ways to ask students like this an important question: "Is it uncomfortable for you right now to be in class while your peers are expressing strong feelings or asking deep questions in class?" This conversation can be facilitated in private, with a school counselor present:

Ted lost his father when he was in 8th grade. According to my colleagues, he had never really expressed his grief. He grew close to his grandfather; then at the beginning of 10th grade, his grandfather died. Ted was in turmoil, but he had strong beliefs about not exposing his grief to others outside his family.

Another student in the class had lost her father the year before. Keisha's way of healing was to talk about her grief whenever she could. She saw our class as a wonderful opportunity to express her feelings and share insights with others about death and grieving.

Ted despised Keisha. I could feel him seething every time she talked. Soon he began to act out in ways that made it harder and harder for our class to hold a meaningful conversation.

It took me months to realize that despite his tough and joking exterior, Ted was in too much pain to be in this particular class. After a conference with his mother and the counselor, we found another way for Ted to fulfill this requirement. Our class never really came together. I felt deep remorse for not acting sooner.

In conferences with the student and sometimes, parents, we can discover if these students need permission to leave during these segments of class and perhaps need a referral for counseling to address their deeper issues. We may also discover that we are dealing with a student who just needs firm, consistent, and caring boundaries that don't allow his or her behavior or opinions to interfere with the class.

In working with all students—even potential saboteurs—we will be most effective when we have discovered our own capacity for caring discipline. When we carry ourselves in a way that conveys respect rather than dominance and that requires respect rather than submission, we learn to set boundaries that protect the whole class. Such boundaries allow the class to go on despite disruptions from one or two other students. Then, after class, we can ensure that the disruptive students receive the care and attention they need.

Words and Deeds of Teachers and Other "Elders"

"I have not been trained as a counselor," protest many teachers. "Why should I encourage students to share feelings in my class?" Or "I can't consider spiritual development in my classroom—the parents would sue me."

Parents are equally wary: "There are very few teachers I would trust with this spiritual stuff—whether it's a fundamentalist zealot or some naive New Ager, I don't want teachers passing their beliefs off on my kid."

I have worked with many colleagues and school leaders who have chosen to confront these dangers with ingenuity and courage. Pooling our creativity, being willing to make mistakes and stay open-minded to those who appear to challenge our credibility, we move from fear and paralysis to finding *safe and appropriate ways* to invite the inner life into schools. When we listen to others and speak with respect, we can collaborate to create curriculums and methodology that will help our students, teachers, and parents honor the soul of education.

The methods described in this book are finding their way into our educational culture in a variety of exciting ways. Teachers from many disciplines and grade levels integrate the methods of "Passages" with their own creative responsiveness to their communities:

• A high school English teacher in an inner-city high school in Washington, D.C., provides art materials for students to symbolically express their feelings, goals, and strengths. As they discuss the assigned literature, they shift periodically into telling stories from their own lives that relate to the struggles of the characters in their books.

• A health educator in Colorado provides a "transitions" course for 9th grade students, weaving social and emotional skills and opportunities for expression together with study skills and health issues. With the students' permission, the health teacher shares the students' "mysteries questions" with the academic faculty, who are awed and amazed by both the "hidden" wisdom and pain in students they see every day. After a year of resisting the idea of initiating a comprehensive program to address heart, soul, and community, this faculty begins to voice enthusiasm and curiosity about next steps.

• An 8th grade English teacher organizes the entire curriculum around the theme of relationship and love, selecting literature that relates to these themes (Trustees of Boston University, 1993). In addition to reading, analytical discussion, and writing, her students keep personal journals to express their own feelings about these themes. Once a week, they sit in "council," relating stories and feelings from their own lives that have been stirred by the required readings. At the end of the year, she designs activities for an 8th grade field trip that will provide a simple but meaningful "rite of passage" from middle school to high school.

• A 2nd grade teacher in New York integrates a sharing circle weekly into her contained classroom, using games, art, and movement to awaken the realm of imagination and soul and help the children make the transition from academic learning to the more vulnerable territory of personal expression.

• A teacher in a prison school on an island off Manhattan introduces the "council" concept to a population that is not only deeply troubled but constantly changing; students come and go weekly, so that consistency is not an option for building safety in the group. "I could not believe the impact!" this teacher reports. "The use of simple ritual made it safe enough for these kids to speak from the heart in a way I've worked for all my career. I felt the shift inside me at our retreat when we teachers spoke to each other in council in a way I never dreamed possible among colleagues. It gave me hope then, and I have even more hope now that I see how my boys respond."

In addition to teachers, many counselors, parents, and community leaders with whom I have worked are using these same methods to bring soul into other group experiences:

• A Spanish teacher in the Bronx takes the curriculum he has learned while teaching the "Senior Passage Course" and translates it into a rites of passage program for the church youth group he leads in his Hispanic community. No one has ever seen the church so full and alive as when parents are invited to church for a ceremony honoring the teenagers when they return from their retreat.

• A counselor of "high-risk" middle school students in one of the most violent communities in the Denver area discovers that "honoring young voices" produces a shift in her work that deeply satisfies this 20-year veteran of the public schools. She finds herself nourishing the souls as well as the psyches of these young people: "I watch my students from diverse backgrounds share such deep human experiences through Council. These are students who would never have connected with one another otherwise. The depth of self-discovery, understanding, and expression in the emotionally safe environment I could facilitate after Passages training is profound."

• A mother of three brings the tools and principles of Passages into a church youth group she cofacilitates. Wrestling with whether it is appropriate to do this work with her own child present, she decides to ask her daughter how she feels. Her daughter replies: "Go for it, Mom, it sounds great! And if I have something too private to share in front of you, I can always talk privately to the other leader."

• Twenty-five members of Congress sit in the basement of the Capitol Building, learning to be coleaders for the first bipartisan retreat for the U.S. Congress. They have completed a ground rules process, and I lead them now in practicing a simplified version of the council process. A month from now, they will guide scores of members through this same process in small groups . "We have never talked like this to one another," says a Congressman from Illinois. "I forgot who is a Democrat and who's Republican. I feel hopeful that we might actually begin to bring civility into this House if other members can experience at the retreat the compassion and respect we've just felt in this room today."

These and many other professionals and parents are seeking ways to encourage the development of heart, spirit, and community. They are learning practices that can invite adults and students alike to engage in the powerful dialogues and meaningful experiences for which we all yearn. There is a beginning of a spiritual renaissance in our modern culture. It cannot come too soon for the next generation.

In a pluralistic society, educators can respect the separation of church and state and still give students a glimpse of the rich array of experiences that feed the soul. We can provide a forum that recognizes and celebrates the ways individual students nourish their spirits. We can offer activities that allow them to feel deeply connected—to themselves, to their family and community, and to the larger world.

Perhaps most important, as teachers, we can honor our students' search for what *they* believe gives meaning and integrity to their lives, and how they can connect to what is most precious for them. In the search itself, in loving the questions, in the deep yearning they let themselves feel, young people can discover what is essential in their own lives and in life itself, and what allows them to bring their own gifts to the world.

References and Bibliography

Arrien, A. (1993). *The four-fold way: Walking the paths of the warrior, teacher, healer and visionary.* San Francisco: HarperSanFrancisco.

Benard, B. (1991). *Fostering resiliency in kids: Protective factors in the family, school, and community.* Portland, OR: Northwest Regional Educational Laboratory.

Bennet, J. G. (1984). A survey of the problem. In J. G. Bennett (Ed.), *The spiritual hunger for the modern child: A series of ten lectures.* Charles Town, WV: Claymont Communications.

Benson, P. (1997). Spirituality and the adolescent journey. *Reclaiming Children and Youth, 5*(4), 206–209, 219.

Berman, S. (1997). *Children's social consciousness and the development of social responsibility.* Albany: State University of New York Press.

Brawer, F. B. (1996, April). Retention-attrition in the nineties. *ERIC Digest* (ED393510). Available on the Internet: http://www.ed.gov/databases/ERIC_Digests/ed393510.html

Brendtro, L., Brokenleg, M., & Van Bockern, S. (1990). *Reclaiming youth at risk: Our hope for the future.* Bloomington, IN: National Education Service.

Caine, R. N., & Caine, G. (1997). *Education on the edge of possibility.* Alexandria, VA: Association for Supervision and Curriculum Development.

Campbell, D. (1997). *The Mozart effect: Tapping the power of music to heal the body, strengthen the mind, and unlock the creative spirit.* New York: Avon Books.

Childerhose, B. (1998). Doing good doing what you love. *Shambhala Sun, 7*(2), 48–49.

A child's ground of discovery: An interview with Margaret Flinsch. (1996, November). *Parabola, 21*(4), 27–33.

Coles, R.(1990). *The spiritual life of children.* Boston: Houghton Mifflin.

Csikszentmihaly, M. (1990). *Flow and the psychology of discovery and invention.* New York: Harper & Row.

Csikszentmihaly, M. (1996). *Creativity.* New York: Harper Collins.

Davis, J., Lockwood, L., & Wright, C. (1991, Winter). Reasons for not reporting peak experiences. *Journal of Humanistic Psychology, 31*(1), 86–94.

Dewey, J. (1933). *How we think: A restatement of the relation of reflective thinking to the educative process.* New York: D.C. Heath.

Dewey, J. (1957). *Reconstruction in philosophy.* New York: Beacon Press.

Elias, M. J., Zins, J. E., Weissberg, R. P., Frey, K. S., Greenberg, M. T., Haynes, N. M., Kessler, R., Schwab-Stone, M. E., & Shriver, T. P. (1997). *Promoting social and emotional learning: Guidelines for educators.* Alexandria, VA: Association for Supervision and Curriculum Development.

Elkind, D. (1981). *The hurried child: Growing up too fast too soon.* Reading, MA: Addison-Wesley.

Foster, S., & Little, M. (1987). The vision quest: Passing from childhood to adulthood. In L. C. Mahdi, S. Foster, & M. Little. (1987). *Betwixt and between: Patterns of masculine and feminine initiation* (pp. 79–110). LaSalle, IL: Open Court Press.

Fowler, J., with Nipkow, K. E., & Schweitzer, F. (1991). *Stages of faith and religious development: Implications for church, education, and society.* New York: Crossroad.

Frankl, V. E. (1984). *Man's search for meaning: An introduction to Logotherapy* (3rd ed.). New York: Simon & Schuster.

Garbarino, J. (1999). *Lost boys: Why our sons turn violent and how we can save them.* New York: The Free Press.

Gardner, H. (1993). *Creating minds.* New York: HarperCollins.

Glazer, S. (Ed.). (1999). *The heart of learning: Spirituality in education.* New York: Tarcher/Putnam.

Goleman, D. (1994, Spring). A great idea in education: Emotional literacy. *Great Ideas in Education: A Unique Book Review and Resource Catalog,* No. 2, pp. 33–34.

Goleman, D. (1995). *Emotional intelligence.* New York: Bantam

Goleman, D., Kaufman, P., & Ray, M. (1992). *The creative spirit.* New York: Dutton.

Gross, V. (1989). *Educating for reverence: The legacy of Abraham Joshua Heschel.* Bristol, IN: Wyndham Hall Press.

Gurian, M. (1998). *A fine young man: What parents, mentors and educators can do to shape adolescent boys into exceptional men.* New York: Tarcher/Putnam.

Halford, J. (1998, December–1999, January). Longing for the sacred in schools: A conversation with Nel Noddings. *Educational Leadership, 56*(4), 28–32.

Hart, P. (1998). *New leadership for a new century: Key findings from a study on youth, leadership, and community service.* Washington, DC: Peter Hart Research Associates, Inc.

Haynes, C., & Nord, W. (1998). *Taking religion seriously across the curriculum.* Alexandria, VA: Association for Supervision and Curriculum Development.

Huizinga, J. (1996, November). What "play" is: Engagement and absorption. *Parabola, 21*(4), 59–63.

Jensen, E. (1998). *Teaching with the brain in mind.* Alexandria, VA: Association for Supervision and Curriculum Development.

Kamperidis, L. (1992, February). Surrounded by water, dying of thirst. *Parabola, 17*(1), 12–17.

Kessler, R. (1998, June). The teaching presence. *Forum,* No. 35, pp. 30–37.

Kessler, R. (1999, December–2000, January). Initiation—saying good-bye to childhood. *Educational Leadership, 57*(4), 30–33.

Kids who kill. (1999, April 21). *Online NewsHour.* Available: http://www.pbs.org/newshour

Lantieri, L., & Patti, J. (1996). *Waging peace in our schools.* Boston: Beacon Press.

Mahdi, L. C., Christopher, N. G., & Meade, M. (1996). *Crossroads: The quest for contemporary rites of passage.* Chicago: Open Court Press.

Mahdi, L. C., Foster, S., & Little, M. (1987). *Betwixt and between: Patterns of masculine and feminine initiation.* LaSalle, IL: Open Court Press.

Mann, L. (1998). Who's in charge? *ASCD Education Update, 40*(6), 1, 4.

McGrath, A. (1998, April 20). Algebra and sympathy. *U.S. News and World Report, 124*(15), 57–58.

McCullough, L. (1996, January/February). Crucible for change. *Common Boundary, 14*(1), 49–51.

Meade, M. (1993). *Men and the water of life: Initiation and the tempering of men.* San Francisco: HarperSanFrancisco.

Merton, T. (1955). *No man is an island.* New York: Harcourt Brace Jovanovich.

Miller, J. P. (1999). *Education and the soul: Towards a spiritual curriculum.* New York: SUNY Press.

Miller, R. (1995–96, Winter). The renewal of education and culture: A multifaceted task. *Great Ideas in Education,* No. 7, p. 5.

Moffett, J. (1994). *The universal schoolhouse: Spiritual awakening through education.* San Francisco: Jossey Bass.

Moore, P. (1996, Spring). Multicultural education: Another look. *Update on Law-Related Education, 20*(2), 22–25.

Moore, T. (1992). *Care of the soul: A guide for cultivating depth and sacredness in everyday life.* New York: HarperCollins.

Nachmanovitch, S. (1990). *Free play: The power of] improvisation in life and the arts.* Los Angeles: Jeremy Tarcher.

Neville, B. (1989). *Educating psyche: Emotion, imagination and the unconscious in learning.* Melbourne, Australia: Collins Dove.

Noddings, N. (1992). *The challenge to care in schools: An alternative approach to education.* New York: Teachers College Press.

Nord, W. (1995). *Religion and American education: Rethinking a national dilemma.* Chapel Hill: University of North Carolina.

Oládélé, F. (1998, December–1999, January). Passing down the spirit. *Educational Leadership, 56*(4), 62–66.

Ostrander, S., & Schroeder, L. (1979). *Super-learning.* New York: Dell.

Palmer, P. (1993). *To know as we are known: Education as a spiritual journey.* San Francisco: HarperSanFrancisco.

Palmer, P. (1995). *The art and craft of formation: A reflective handbook for the formation programs of the Fetzer Institute.* Unpublished manuscript, Draft #3.

Palmer, P. (1998). *The courage to teach: Exploring the inner landscape of a teacher's life.* San Francisco: Jossey-Bass.

Palmer, P. (1998, December–1999, January). Evoking the spirit in public education. *Educational Leadership, 56*(4), 6–11.

Pasley, M. (Ed.). (1973). *Selections English: Shorter works of Franz Kafka.* London: Seher & Warburg.

Peterson, J. W. (1987). *The secret life of kids: An exploration into their psychic senses.* Wheaton, IL: Quest Books, Theosophical Publishing House.

Pool, C. (1997, March). Maximizing learning: A conversation with Renate Nummela Caine. *Educational Leadership, 54*(6), 11–15.

Rilke, R. M. (1962). *Letters to a young poet.* (M. D. Herter Norton, Trans.). New York: W.W. Norton.

Romano, M. (1999, May 19). Problem is hate, youth tells Congress. *Denver Rocky Mountain News,* A4.

Schweitzer, A. (1949, October). Your second job. *Readers Digest, 55,* 1–5.

Shriver, T. P., & Weissberg, R. P. (1996, May 15). No new wars! *Education Week,* pp. 33, 37.

Simms, L. (1998). Through the story's terror—In the heart of the tale's protagonist. *Parabola, 23*(3), 46–53.

Sloan, D. (1994, Fall/Winter). Exploring the spiritual foundations of education. *Renewal: A Journal for Waldorf Education,* pp. 11–15.

Somé, M. (1994, July/August). Rites of passage. *Utne Reader,* No. 64, pp. 67–68.

The Spirit of Education. (1998, December–1999, January). *Educational Leadership* (Entire Issue), *56*(4).

Stahl, R. J. (1994). Using "think-time" and "wait-time" skillfully in the classroom. ERIC Digest. (ERIC Document No: ED370885).

Sternberg, R. J. (1997, March). What does it mean to be smart? *Educational Leadership, 56*(4), 20–24.

Storr, A. (1965). Churchill's black dog, Kafka's mice, and other phenomena of the human mind. New York: Grove Press.

Storr, A. (1988). *Solitude: A return to the self.* New York: Ballantine, Free Press.

Sylwester, R. (1995). *A celebration of neurons: An educator's guide to the human brain.* Alexandria, VA: Association for Supervision and Curriculum Development.

Trustees of Boston University. (1993). *The art of loving well: A character education curriculum for today's teenagers.* Boston: Boston University, School of Education.

Turnbull, C. (1983). *The human cycle.* New York: Simon & Schuster.

Turner, V. (1987). Betwixt and between: the liminal period in rites of passage. In L. C. Mahdi, S. Foster, & M. Little (Eds.), *Betwixt and between: Patterns of masculine and feminine initiation.* LaSalle, IL: Open Court Press.

Viadero, D. (1997, May 7). Adventure programs found to have lasting positive impact. *Education Week, 16*(32), 8.

Ward, A. Y. (1996, July/August). The question of life. *Common Boundary, 14*(4), 30–35.

Weaver, R., & Cotrell, H. (1992). A non-religious spirituality that causes students to clarify their values and to respond with passion. *Education, 112*(3), 426–435.

Wesley, D. (1998, December–1999, January). Believing in our students. *Educational Leadership, 56*(4), 42–45.

Wolf, A. (1996). *Nurturing the spirit: In non-sectarian classrooms.* Hollidaysburg, PA: Parent Child Press.

Wood, C. (1999). *Time to teach, time to learn: Changing the pace of school.* Greenfield, MA: Northeast Foundation for Children, Inc.

Zimmerman, J., & Coyle, V. (1996). *The way of council.* Las Vegas, NV: Bramble Books.

Zweig, C., & Abrams, J. (1991). *Meeting the shadow: The hidden power of the dark side of human nature.* Los Angeles: J. P. Tarcher.

Index

177

About the Author

Rachael Kessler is the director of The Institute for Social and Emotional Learning, where she consults on curriculum, staff training, and organizational development for schools, communities and individual educators. Her focus has been integrating heart, spirit, and community into the classroom and empowering educators to create constructive rites of passage for adolescents. Called by Daniel Goleman in the *New York Times* a "leader in a new movement for emotional literacy," Kessler is also a coauthor of *Promoting Social and Emotional Learning: Guidelines for Educators* (ASCD, 1997), the author of numerous articles, and producer and publisher of the 1992 video *Honoring Young Voices: A Vision for Education*.

Kessler also works with her husband, Mark Gerzon, to conduct training on facilitating community building and constructive dialogue in highly polarized settings. Their primary clients are educational and civic leaders, including the U.S. Congress. In 1997 and 1999, Kessler and Gerzon provided a design, training, and facilitation for the first and second Bipartisan Congressional Retreat. She is also the mother of three young men: Shane, Ari, and Mikael Gerzon-Kessler.

To contact the author or receive information on training, consultation, or other publications, write to The Institute for Social and Emotional Learning, 3833 North 57th Street, Boulder, CO 80301 (URL: http://www.mediatorsFoundation.org/soulofed; e-mail: selrachael@aol.com). (Please note the second "a" in rachael for the correct e-mail address.)